FOLIAGE

— FOR —

YEAR ROUND

COLOUR

Photographs by Clive Nichols

Jane Taylor

WARD LOCK

ACKNOWLEDGEMENTS

All photographs by Clive Nichols, except those on pages
50, 57 and 100 which are by Jane Taylor. Line drawings
by Mike Shoebridge.

A WARD LOCK BOOK

First published in the UK 1995
by Ward Lock, Villiers House, 41/47 Strand, LONDON WC2N 5JE

A Cassell Imprint

Copyright © Text Jane Taylor 1995

Distributed in the United States
by Sterling Publishing Co., Inc.
387 Park Avenue South, New York, NY 10016-8810

Distributed in Australia
by Capricorn Link (Australia) Pty Ltd
2/13 Carrington Road, Castle Hill NSW 2154

A British Library Cataloguing in Publication Data block for this book
may be obtained from the British Library

ISBN 0 7063 7210 7
Typeset by Litho Link Ltd, Welshpool, Powys, Wales
Printed and bound in Spain by Cronion S.A., Barcelona

CONTENTS

CHAPTER 1

PAINTING GARDEN PICTURES WITH FOLIAGE

F EW GARDENERS WOULD want to dispense with flowers altogether but, for satisfying, enduring garden pictures, you can't beat leaves. Their diversity is extraordinary, from the tiny needles of heathers to the huge, rough leaves of *Gunnera manicata*, from the swords of iris or phormium to the feathery sprays of mimosa, from the finely dissected fronds of ferns to the wide dinner-plates of hostas. Leaves can make wonderful compositions in their own right, using form and density and texture in counterpoint. They are with us for much longer than flowers; in temperate climates at least, hardly any flowers carry on non-stop for four to five months, let alone all year, as do evergreens. Leaves are an essential part of the framework and backdrop of the garden, the setting for the more transient beauty of flowers.

This book, above all, is about colour from foliage. Green is also a colour, and it is only lack of space that obliges me to concentrate on leaves that are other than green; nevertheless I cannot pass by green without a quick reminder of its diversity. The fundamental distinction to be drawn is between the greens that lean towards blue and those that belong with yellow. Jade, viridian and aqua are blue-greens; pea, lettuce and chartreuse are yellow-greens, and so, at the darker end of the scale, is olive – the colour of the unripe fruit, that is, not the silvery grey of the leaves of an olive tree. In between are the neutral greens, or mid-greens, in which neither yellow nor blue dominates. There are greens so dark that they are almost black – those of yew, *Helleborus foetidus*, even ivy – and others that are pale and fresh – *Hosta plantaginea*, the velvety-soft, pleated fans of *Alchemilla mollis*, the young spears of day lilies.

As well as green in all its variations, leaves come in a range of colours almost as wide as that of flowers themselves. There are leaves that are so densely felted with hairs that they are platinum- or silver-pale, almost white, and others that are so deep a purple or mahogany that they are virtually black; leaves coated with a waxy finish that gives them a blue cast; yellow leaves, chartreuse leaves, copper,

Fig 1 Gunnera manicata *has the largest leaves of any hardy perennial – in maturity, they are big enough to stand beneath.*

mahogany, bronze, beetroot and plum-maroon leaves, leaves variegated with white or cream or yellow and some jazzy leaves that mix pink and red and yellow and white. There are leaves that are vivid in spring before fading to green summer respectability and leaves that have their moment of glory in autumn as they flare into bonfire colours before falling. Some leaves turn to rich colours – old gold, crimson, plum or blackcurrant purple – with the winter cold, and a few appear in winter, going to ground in summer.

Juxtaposing plants of similar colouring but different texture or outline makes for some striking effects. Imagine a scheme of lime, chartreuse and chrome yellow and mossy greens, using broad-leaved hostas, grasses and sedges, with their rapier-fine blades, and a golden mock orange, all in the dappled shadow of the golden honey locust, *Gleditsia triacanthos* 'Sunburst'. Out in the glare of the sun, a gravel-dressed bed of silvers and greys would give an entirely different impression, with the silver threads of *Artemisia splendens*, the low mat of grey Prince-of-Wales feathers of *Tanacetum densum* ssp. *amani*, the tight bobbles of santolinas and, arising perhaps from a carpet of the silver-sheened, violet-purple of *Tradescantia pallida* (syn. *Setcreasea purpurea*), the amazing hemisphere of vivid glaucous-blue stilettos of *Yucca whipplei*.

And that leads me to an important caveat. It is all too easy, faced with the marvellous abundance of colourful and variegated foliage plants available to us today, to overdo them. They make strong statements and can lead to a feeling of freneticism that is the very antithesis of what we need in our gardens today: peace, tranquillity, repose. Use them sparingly; create dramatic groupings by all means, but allow for quiet expanses of grey or cool, glaucous foliage as well, and use plenty of the subtle shades of green – olive, apple, moss, almond, sage. The sense

Few trees colour so brilliantly in autumn as the Japanese maples. With their graceful habit and dainty, fingered leaves, they earn their keep in summer too.

of drama will be enhanced if the eye can also light on a soothing and harmonious planting before the next striking encounter.

FOLIAGE AS THE SETTING FOR FLOWERS

Whatever your style of gardening, every plant you grow is seen in a context. That context can make or mar the picture you seek to create. Foliage, even green foliage, is not just some kind of neutral background; it is very much part of the picture, with an important role to play. Think of one of the most common elements of the spring garden: pink flowering cherries. Their mauve-tinted pink calls for a backdrop in the blue-influenced half of the spectrum: the very opposite of the sharp greens of much spring foliage. Instead, imagine a pink cherry against a background of blue-grey or dark blue-green conifers. Immediately the pink loses crudeness and gains depth. Later that same backdrop can make the ideal setting for lilacs or the crimson hawthorn.

The yellow of forsythia, and of the laburnum that follows it, is more appropriately partnered by a green that leans towards yellow. This need not be a light green; some dark greens belong in the yellow half of the spectrum too, as you will immediately see if you compare the foliage of the incense cedar, *Calocedrus decurrens*, with that of the Japanese white pine, *Pinus parviflora*. Both are dark green but the first is yellow-based, the second blue-based.

This group of three, easy-going perennials makes a year-round picture, contrasting the leathery, evergreen leaves of Bergenia 'Morgenröte', the woolly Stachys byzantina 'Silver Carpet' and the fleshy, blue-green foliage of Sedum 'Herbstfreude' ('Autumn Joy'), here in full, dusky-pink flower.

Silvers and greys

If the above is true of the most universal of foliage colours, green, how much more true it is of 'coloured' leaves. Imagine a border of silver and grey foliage and think of the different values it will give to glowing orange, pale primrose, shades of pink and mauve, or to white. Yellow leaves – usually called 'golden' though they are almost invariably much nearer to chartreuse or lime, butter or buttercups – make one kind of statement if you ally them with yellow flowers but quite another with blue, sharp sunset colours, or crimson, burgundy and purple.

Purple, mahogany and bronze

Purple foliage – which is almost always some shade of maroon, madder or chocolate brown, rather than the reddish violet to which the word 'purple' properly refers – contrasts dramatically with yellow foliage, more subtly with glaucous blue or grey. As a setting for flowers, purple foliage will take: yellow, especially the softer, lemon or primrose yellows; crimson, for richness; scarlet and vermilion, as in the famous red borders at Hidcote; pink and mauve, maybe with some grey foliage in the group as well; white, of course; and, most intriguingly of all, flowers of brown and madder colouring on a pale ground, where the deeper tones of the flower match the foliage behind.

Variegations

Variegated foliage is so diverse that it is hard to generalize. It ranges from the understated – a fine marginal line of white, cream or yellow, or subdued marbling – to the blatant, where one or more, strongly contrasting colours make the leaf as bright as a flower. In variegated monocots (the term for plants with only one seed leaf) the stripes, in all but the rarest of exceptions, run vertically along the leaf, which is often spear-shaped or rapier-fine. Hostas are also monocots and most have very broad leaves; their variegations tend to have some relationship with the veining of the leaf, which gives them a kind of logic not always present in dicots (generally broad-leaved plants with two seed leaves). A variegation which consists of blotches and speckles can look messy but sometimes works, as with the best of the spotted laurels. As well as adding colour, variegations can often redeem an otherwise boring leaf that, in its normal form, is a mid-green of undistinguished outline; hebes, phlox and mock orange are examples of this.

It is easy to overdo variegations and it takes great skill to make a border solely of variegated plants and not end up with visual indigestion. A single variegated plant can be a star in its own right, of course, but it can also be the setting for a flower that will thereby be thrown into greater relief. Because flowers on the whole are short-lived, you can contrive changing seasonal effects. Imagine a white-variegated shrubby dogwood, *Cornus alba* 'Elegantissima'. Use it to host a violet-blue clematis and, for the period of the clematis' flowering, it will draw the eye to itself and away from the dogwood, which becomes its setting and context, showing off the rich blue flowers in a way that a plain green shrub would not.

You can play with flower colour and foliage, too, by matching flower colour and season. *Caryopteris* × *clandonensis* has violet-blue flowers and, ordinarily, greyish foliage, but it has a form 'Worcester Gold', in which the foliage is a luminescent chartreuse yellow. You could add a late-flowering, soft-blue clematis in a neighbouring host, encouraging a few stems to trail over the caryopteris as well. The principal host could itself have yellow or yellow-variegated foliage (a golden conifer or *Elaeagnus* × *ebbingei* 'Limelight', perhaps); or you could choose instead a host with blue-toned foliage (a blue-grey conifer or *Berberis temolaica* maybe), depending on whether you wanted to emphasize the cool or the sunny element of the planting.

MAKING PATTERNS WITH FOLIAGE PLANTS

So far, I have thought in fairly conventional terms about the sort of garden you might already have and want to enhance with foliage plants, or perhaps the garden you do not yet have and would like to create. But you could also use many of the same plants in a much more adventurous way. You could experiment by planting them in geometrically exact patterns of formal shapes, or in controlled, interlocking swirls and spirals of colour, to make abstract patterns – a kind of permanent, modernistic bedding inspired by the tropical plantings of Roberto

Opposite: *The tiny, golden leaves of* Lonicera nitida *'Baggesen's Gold' contrast with the bolder, rounded, ruby-purple foliage of* Cotinus coggygria *'Purpurea'*.

Burle Marx but, unlike virtually all conventional bedding, potentially at its brightest and best in winter. Like Victorian carpet bedding, generous quantities of each kind of plant are needed to make a bold statement about the colour and texture of each band, square or swirl.

This is not a style suited to every type of garden. For a start, consider the house you live in. An old cottage, with its picturesque irregularities, might look quite incongruous in a setting more reminiscent of an abstract painting than of a traditional English garden. But a formal knot garden worked out in coloured foliage might work very well. If, like the less fortunate majority of us, you live in a twentieth-century house of no particular distinction, you might as well give it some style and cachet by creating a stunning and unusual garden around it. You could take up the suggestion of the British gardening writer and broadcaster, Roger Grounds, for a formal front garden like a giant chess board, with black squares of *Ophiopogon planiscapus* 'Nigrescens' and white squares of *Holcus mollis* 'Variegatus', surrounded by a clipped border of plain green dwarf box, *Buxus*

Even the humble golden privet, Ligustrum ovalifolium *'Aureum', is transformed when it hosts the nodding, blue lanterns of spring-flowering* Clematis macropetala.

Fig 2 *The strap-shaped leaves of* Ophiopogon planiscapus *'Nigrescens' are as near to black as any plant can be.*

sempervirens 'Suffruticosa', alternating with the white-variegated *B. sempervirens* 'Elegantissima'. Or, if you have a curving drive, you could follow and elaborate on its curves.

Variations on a theme

A scheme of this kind could be carried out with heathers and conifers, using pencil-slim or pyramidal conifers to make vertical accents. Instead of the rather clichéd 'natural' arrangement of heathers-plus-conifers (which is doubly incongruous if it is contrived in a small suburban garden), and if you want to include some of the striking, but thoroughly unnatural, coloured-foliage varieties, you can use exactly the same materials in a way that exploits the very quality which makes these plants so unlike their wild forebears.

Another way of exploiting the tension between similar outlines and textures and varied colours is to design an abstract scheme using only coloured grasses. There still remain some grassy-leaved plants among the perennials – *Acorus*, *Liriope* and *Ophiopogon* spring to mind. Again, there are plenty of options for low carpets and tall accents using only grasses. You could make a wide sweep of one of the little blue fescues (*Festuca*) and set a clump of the like-coloured *Helictotrichon sempervirens* or *Elymus glaucus* to soar above them, or contrast the blue carpet with a tall accent of gold, purple or white-variegated grass. You could also make adjoining bands of blue and blood red, gold, bronze and chocolate, and white; not to mention the many ornamental grasses in shades of green, that I have not listed here.

CHAPTER 2

THE BONES OF THE GARDEN

GARDENS ARE NEVER STATIC. In temperate regions, the passage of the seasons is marked by the unfurling of leaves in spring, the mature foliage of summer, autumn colour and the carpets of fallen leaves underfoot, and by the contrasts of bare branches and of evergreens in winter. Within this unending cycle, there are some plants that are in good leaf all year round. They are the invaluable backbone of the garden, a solid presence amid the transience of flower, fruit and falling leaves.

Evergreens, just as much as plants that lose their leaves in winter, change with the seasons, but they do so differently: their new growths emerge pale or bright against a backdrop of their own older, darker leaves, maturing during summer and perhaps flushing to rich, warm tones in winter. The plants that earn inclusion in this chapter always look good and are never boring.

STAR TURNS

The golden-variegated elaeagnus are prime examples of plants that hold the stage all year round. In winter *Elaeagnus pungens* 'Maculata' is bright as daffodils with its dark green leaves splashed with yellow. In spring its new growths are hazed with the faint, metallic scurf that characterizes the genus; this is even more pronounced in those of the newer and more desirable *E.* × *ebbingei* 'Limelight' (with central golden variegation) and 'Gilt Edge'. From winter brightness, they pass to greater subtlety in spring and early summer. It is perhaps too early to be sure about *Escallonia* 'Gold Brian', a recent introduction; its all-gold leaves are bright, to be sure, and its growth fairly compact.

Another cheerful evergreen, that old favourite, the spotted laurel, *Aucuba japonica*, deserves better than a place in a dusty, town shrubbery. A rounded, leafy shrub, it comes in several forms: freckled or blotched with yellow, as in 'Gold Dust' and 'Crotonifolia'; or with solid yellow markings – 'Picturata', with a central splash of gold, and 'Sulphurea Marginata' broadly edged with soft yellow. If paired with a male, females will also bear scarlet fruits. All these except 'Picturata' are female, as is the original introduction ('Variegata', formerly 'Maculata') with its more sparsely freckled leaves.

Heathers, conifers and brightly variegated forms of Euonymus fortunei *defy the seasons in this island bed.*

In mild gardens, especially by the sea, *Griselinia littoralis* is always appealing with its large, soap-smooth, apple-green leaves. Its cream-variegated forms – 'Bantry Bay', 'Dixon's Cream' and ivory-margined 'Variegata' – are among the most choice of variegated evergreens, the combination of pale green and cream more subtle than showy on close inspection but wonderfully bright from a distance.

More frost-resistant than this is *Ligustrum lucidum*, a large shrub or small tree with evergreen leaves, glossy and dark as a camellia's, obtainable in two desirable, variegated forms as well: 'Excelsum Superbum' with yellow and cream variegations, and 'Tricolor' with narrower leaves bordered white with a hint of pink in youth. It is the touches of pink to blackcurrant purple in its cream margins, enhanced by burgundy-red leaf stalks, that give a special allure to the variegated Portugal laurel, *Prunus lusitanica* 'Variegata'. The cherry laurel, *P. laurocerasus*, also has a variegated form, known as 'Castlewellan' or 'Marbled White', to describe the heavy mottling and splashes of cream on glossy green.

Holly is handsome all year with its shining, dark foliage. *Ilex aquifolium* is the common holly and has given rise to many variants with white-, cream- or yellow-variegated leaves. One of the best is the hybrid *I. × altaclarensis* 'Lawsoniana', whose large and mostly spineless leaves are splashed with gold at the centre.

Hollies and griselinia can be clipped if necessary, as can that other seaside favourite, *Euonymus japonicus*. However, if they are to be the focus of attention they are best left free-growing. Unless grown as a hedge, and sometimes even then, the euonymus is usually seen in one of its white- or yellow-variegated forms. The most striking of all is *E. japonicus* 'Latifolius Albomarginatus' with broad leaves splashed with grey and boldly margined in ivory white.

There is a surprising number of plants with leaves like holly, among them *Osmanthus heterophyllus*, a rounded, glossy-foliaged evergreen that has given rise to some appealing variants. 'Aureomarginatus' has leaves margined with yellow, while 'Variegatus' is quieter with its ivory-white margins and grey marbling. Brightest of them is 'Goshiki' ('Tricolor'), with white and coral-pink variegations. The pink tones of *Photinia davidiana* 'Palette' lean more towards rose, especially in spring; later the bold cream splashes are prominent.

There are not many purple-leaved evergreens suitable for cool temperate climates. Among them is *Berberis × stenophylla* 'Claret Cascade', which has the same spraying habit and small, almost needle-like leaves of the type but with the younger foliage wine purple against the purple-green of the older leaves.

The firethorns, or pyracanthas, are usually chosen for their bright berries, but there are two variegated pyracanthas that I know of: 'Sparkler', with small leaves edged white, very aptly named; and 'Harlequin', with cream, pink and green foliage. In close-up it is very distinct but from a distance, the pink is almost invisible, so the effect is of another brightly white-variegated shrub. *Berberis × stenophylla* 'Pink Pearl' is a curious chameleon of a shrub, with some shoots green and others almost wholly pink and cream; the flowers on the green shoots are the usual orange and on the pink shoots they are creamy lemon.

Mainly for sheltered gardens

Pink tints do not always improve a variegated shrub: to my eye, *Pittosporum* 'Garnettii' is spoiled, not enhanced, by the rose-red spotting on its cream-variegated leaves. There are several other variegated pittosporums of greater appeal to choose from; most are selections of *P. tenuifolium*, which has neat, wavy-edged leaves on black stems. Among them are 'Silver Queen', with leaves margined white to give a pale, silvery effect, and 'Irene Patterson', whose leaves are so heavily splashed and flecked with white that it looks as though it has been out in a snowstorm. Others have all-yellow foliage – 'Golden King', 'Warnham Gold', 'Winter Sunshine' – or green splashed with yellow, as in 'Abbotsbury Gold'. 'Wendle Channon' has lime-yellow foliage tinted with red. All grow best in mild areas but are perhaps a little hardier than *P. eugenioïdes* 'Variegatum', a lovely thing with pale green leaves margined cream. The tobira, *P. tobira*, in both

Opposite: *The names of ornamental hollies can be confusing – this one,* Ilex aquifolium *'Golden Queen', is male and will never berry, but with its smartly yellow-variegated foliage, it is striking year round just the same.*

plain, glossy green and variegated form, is more of a spreading, hummocky shrub, the latter very handsome with its whorls of leaves broadly margined white. Also for mild areas is the variegated Chilean myrtle, *Luma apiculata* (syn. *Myrtus apiculatus*) 'Glanleam Gold', a compact evergreen with small, dark green leaves broadly margined gold.

Although it is very slow-growing, *Azara microphylla* 'Variegata' is a star from the start. It has the same fan-like sprays of foliage as the green form but each tiny leaf is variegated with cream. In time it will make a small tree in mild areas, gleaming pale from a distance and intricately patterned when seen close at hand. Another antipodean evergreen that always attracts comment is *Pseudowintera colorata*, in which the leaves are naturally coloured, not green. The upper surface is pale metallic gold, touched with pink and plum, and the reverse is glaucous white.

Among purple-leaved evergreens for milder regions there are *Pittosporum tenuifolium* 'Purpureum', in glittering black-purple, and the purple hop bush, *Dodonaea viscosa* 'Purpurea', which has long, finger-like leaves of reddish-maroon tint. Even more gleaming and highly polished than the pittosporum is *Coprosma* 'Coppershine', which has broad, coppery-bronze leaves. Among the variants of the tea tree, *Leptospermum scoparium*, are some with dusky foliage; one of the best is 'Nicholsii', with bronze-purple needle-leaves and deep crimson flowers. *Leptospermum lanigerum*, by contrast, has tiny grey leaves; 'Silver Sheen' is even better, with larger, silvery-silky leaves.

Evergreen trees

If you want something that will quickly grow to tree stature, you could plant a eucalyptus. Several are resistant to quite severe frosts and in mild regions, the choice is very wide. If you do not prune *Eucalyptus gunnii* hard each year to persuade it to produce its round, blue juvenile foliage, it will make a tree with sickle-shaped, grey-green leaves. As a tree, a better choice would be *E. coccifera*, which has glaucous foliage, or the lovely *E. niphophila*, with its quite large, grey-green leaves and peeling, python-skin bark. The spinning gum, *E. perriniana*, is so called because each pair of rounded, blue-grey leaves is joined at the base to encircle the stem; with time they work loose and spin around in the breeze.

Rhododendrons with lovely leaves – and their companions

For gardeners blessed with leafy, lime-free soil and shelter from searing winds, the rhododendron tribe offer some of the finest year-round foliage plants. What gives several wild species their special appeal is their indumentum, the coloured, felt- or suede-textured reverse to the leaf. They range in size from shrubs to almost tree stature, so one could be fitted into the smallest garden.

There are even some variegated rhododendrons, including *Rhododendron ponticum* 'Variegatum', which has the usual pointed leaves, but margined with cream. 'President Roosevelt' is variegated with yellow; when it flowers the combination of shocking pink trusses with the green and yellow leaves is decidedly painful to the eye. Some people love it.

It is a relief to turn to the wild species, with their grace and poise. One of the

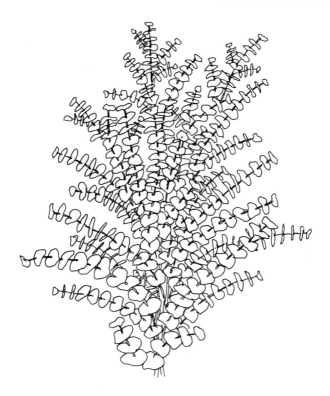

Fig 3 Eucalyptus perriniana *earns its nickname, the spinning gum, from the way the stem-encircling leaves work loose with time and spin in the wind.*

best among the smaller and hardier species is *R. bureaui*, a compact mound of dark, polished leaves, backed with rich mahogany-red felt; the young growths are bright rust red. Smaller and even more slow-growing is *R. haematodes*, with a thick, fox-red felting to the backs of the leaves, and scarlet flowers as a bonus. The scarlet-flowered hybrid rhododendron 'May Day' also has rusty-red suede leaf backs.

If you have space for something larger there is *R. arboreum* 'Sir Charles Lemon', the dark green leaves of which, backed with mahogany felt, contrast with deep red stems and white flowers. *R. campanulatum*, a rather large shrub with fawn suede reverses to the leaves, has a subspecies, *aeruginosum,* with silvery-blue young growths. A few rhododendrons have strikingly glaucous-blue foliage all year; among them *R. cinnabarinum*, with ochre-yellow flowers, and R. *oreotrephes*, with lilac-pink trusses. They look well with the 90 cm (3 ft) hybrid rhododendron 'Elizabeth Lockhart', which has dark purple foliage.

If your soil is suitable for rhododendrons, you will also be able to grow camellias. Almost all camellias, especially those belonging to *Camellia japonica*, have good, glossy, evergreen foliage. There are variegated camellias, for example *C.* x *williamsii* 'Golden Spangles', the rather narrow leaves of which are splashed with yellow. Far more beautiful than this is *Cleyera japonica* 'Fortunei', which also belongs to the tea family. It is best grown in mild areas, where it reaches 1.5 m

(5 ft); its pointed leaves are a dark, polished green, marbled with cream and grey and margined pink and rose. Much more widely known, and hardier, is the jazzy *Leucothoë fontanesiana* 'Rainbow', a low, spreading evergreen with glossy leaves splashed cream, pink, bronze and yellow.

Conifers for centre stage

With rare exceptions, conifers are such good year-rounders that it is difficult to select just a few that are eye-catching, both in colour and in silhouette, all year round. These are plants that have the quality to be chosen as centrepieces.

For many people, the first choice would be a blue spruce. The best of them are a really startling, bright blue-silver. The story begins with *Picea pungens* 'Glauca', or more accurately the Glauca group, for these are seed-raised, about one quarter of them coming blue enough to earn the name Glauca. Most can become large in time but the choicer cultivars, propagated by grafting, tend to grow more slowly, making conical trees that will overtop you in about ten years; as they mature they develop the slightly dipping branches typical of Christmas trees. Among the first were 'Koster' and 'Moerheimii'; a newer cultivar is the more silvery 'Hoopsii'. 'Hoto' is one of the bluest and its dense growth seldom needs pruning, whereas the others may need a little encouragement at first to form the perfect symmetrical cone.

More blue conifers

Almost as blue as these are some forms of the Arizona cypress, *Cupressus arizonica*, with their finer foliage, giving a more feathery effect at a distance. One of the bluest is 'Blue Ice'. They are well adapted to hot, dry climates, where their powdery grey-blue colouring is in tune with the dusty landscape. They are, on the whole, faster-growing than the blue spruces.

Few conifers are so variable as the Lawson's cypresses. *Chamaecyparis lawsoniana* 'Pembury Blue' is outstandingly blue, with steely tints rather than the silvery tints of the spruces. It grows to about 3 m (10 ft) in its first decade, ultimately reaching three times that height, and is of narrowly pyramidal outline. The well-known 'Triomf van Boskoop' is far too big for the average garden but very effective with its glaucous grey-blue foliage. For something more manageable, there is 'Chilworth Silver', a broad, 3 m (10 ft) column of pale silvery blue.

You need a mild climate for the Kashmir cypress, *Cupressus torulosa* 'Cashmeriana', to thrive; or you can grow it in a greenhouse, at least until it gets too big. Where it will grow, it is one of the most beautiful of conifers, a pyramid of weeping branches decked with long, slender, hanging branchlets of intense blue-grey. The Mexican *Pinus ayacahuite*, also best suited to gentler climates, is a beautiful tall pine, with great, blue-grey brushes of long needles.

Juniperus scopulorum 'Skyrocket' makes a slender column of steely blue-grey (fatter in warmer climates). 'Moonglow' is bluer and slightly broader and 'Blue Heaven' is more of a pyramid than a pencil in silhouette. These strong verticals are often associated with flat carpets of heathers but I think they call for some rounded, cloudy outlines as well to soften the contrast.

A fine, symmetrical specimen of the blue spruce, Picea pungens *'Koster' keeps its vivid blue colouring year round, contrasting in spring and summer with the lacy, golden-green foliage of* Gleditsia triacanthos *'Sunburst'.*

The sunny shades of gold

Among the golden conifers fit for a leading role, as with the blues, there is a choice of outlines and of texture. The grey-blue Korean fir has a golden counterpart in *Abies koreana* 'Flava' (also known as 'Aurea'), slow-growing to 1.2 m (4 ft) and with the same broadly triangular outline but yellow, not grey, needles, at their brightest in winter. For year-round value it is hard to better *Cryptomeria japonica* 'Sekkan Sugi', a neat and slender pyramid which changes with the seasons and the angle at which the sun's rays strike, now lemon, now clotted-cream pale, sometimes bronzed or old gold, sometimes new-minted.

The upright, candle-flame or narrowly conical outline of the typical Lawson's cypress is welcome as a strong vertical in the garden and, when that vertical is a bright and cheering golden yellow all year, it can easily become the dominant note. The ideal setting is plenty of mid- to dark greenery. The classic narrow pyramid is *Chamaecyparis lawsoniana* 'Lane' (also known as 'Lanei'), which has rather feathery foliage of a bright, clear yellow. Although tall, it takes comparatively little lateral space; less than 'Stewartii', which has flattened, fern-like sprays of bright, rich yellow on elegantly arching branch tips. 'Moonshine' is a more recent selection with lacy, very bright foliage; it makes a dense, pyramid.

The Monterey cypress, *Cupressus macrocarpa*, is a massive, dark green tree; it too has sported to golden forms, of which two are outstanding: 'Donard Gold' and 'Goldcrest'. Both have feathery-seeming foliage of clear yellow, rather paler in 'Goldcrest', and grow to columnar trees of 9 m (30 ft) or so. There is a golden form of the Italian cypress, *C. sempervirens*: 'Swane's Gold' is a compact column of greenish gold. None of these is at its best in very cold regions and all need some shelter but not shade, which tips their colouring towards green.

If these vertical conifers are too big for your purposes, there are golden forms of both the Irish yew and the Chinese juniper to choose from. The yew, *Taxus baccata* 'Standishii', slowly reaches 1.5 m (5 ft) or more and is very slender in youth, with broad golden needles on a narrow column of a bush, but suffers a bit from middle-aged spread. *Juniperus chinensis* 'Aurea' remains slim all its days, slow-growing and displaying several shades of gold at once, from the pale tints of the new growths to the deepest yellow of the mature foliage. The very variable common juniper, *J. communis*, has a cultivar, 'Gold Cone', which describes itself.

The golden deodar, *Cedrus deodara* 'Aurea', is at its most vivid in spring, fading gradually to lime yellow. It brings a softer-looking touch to the garden, with its longish needles and graceful habit. The appeal of *Chamaecyparis obtusa* 'Crippsii' lies in its rich golden to chartreuse yellow colouring and in its characteristic shape – a loose cone composed of wide, frond-like sprays of foliage. It forms a small tree in time.

Clothing walls

Walls can look beautiful year-round if you make foliage, not flowers, your priority. I shall sing the praises of *Trachelospermum jasminoïdes* 'Variegatum' in Chapter 7, but remind you here that it is a real all-rounder (and has fragrant flowers, too). You might not think of euonymuses and ivies in this context, yet several are outstanding on walls as well as on the flat.

There are two splendid forms of the large-leaved *Hedera colchica*: 'Dentata Variegata' with bold primrose-yellow margins, and 'Sulphur Heart' ('Paddy's Pride'), which of course has the yellow at the centre of the leaf. *H. algeriensis* 'Gloire de Marengo' is not quite so large in leaf and a bit tender, so wall protection suits it. The foliage is subtly variegated with white on grey and pale jade, with pinkish tints in youth.

Candidates for containers

There is much to be said for growing your star year-rounders in containers. You can move them around with the seasons to catch just the aspect they need – sun at one time, shelter and a modicum of shade at another – so that they are always at their best. You can ring the changes with their companions.

Against the boldly variegated, evergreen leaves of the Persian ivy, Hedera colchica *'Dentata Variegata', the year's pageant of flowers unfolds, beginning with snowdrops in winter.*

An ideal all-year shrub for containers is the golden Mexican orange, *Choisya ternata* 'Sundance'. The plain green form is handsome at all times, with its rich green, glossy, blunt-ended, fingered leaves; but it is quite a big shrub and would quickly outgrow a container. The same basic leaf shape and the same rounded outline are shared by the golden form, which is smaller and slower-growing. It has become so popular so quickly that already some people are denigrating it but, given the right setting, with some shelter to keep the bright foliage from scorching, it is first-rate.

Most hollies grow large in time but some make good container plants. An evergreen shrub that everyone except me seems to love is *Hebe × franciscana* 'Variegata' – a neat (I nearly said smug), rounded plant with oblong leaves, broadly margined creamy white, set with geometric precision along the branches. Stubby mauve flower spikes appear in no great quantity at odd times of the year. My preference for a variegated hebe would be 'Carnea Variegata', less dumpy in growth, with longer, narrower leaves, cream and green flushed with pink in winter; the flowers are wands of pink. 'Amanda Cook' is slightly shorter in growth, with broadly cream-margined leaves flushed purple.

Many of the smaller and most colourful conifers are ideal container plants. Instead of being lost amid faster-growing plants in the open ground, they sit cosily in their own individual pots and, when the larger forms eventually outgrow their containers, they can be planted out at a size sufficient to make an immediate impact. Bun-like or domed conifers – such as *Thuja plicata* 'Stoneham Gold', its golden foliage tipped with bronze, the tight, chartreuse-yellow dome of *T. orientalis* 'Aurea Nana', *Chamaecyparis obtusa* 'Nana Lutea', with its ferny, yellow-gold sprays, or the miniature, yellow Lawson's cypress, *C. lawsoniana* 'Minima Aurea' – could be grouped with blue-grey *Abies concolor* 'Compacta' or the ever-popular *C. pisifera* 'Boulevard', its pale, steely grey-blue foliage just tinted with mauve in winter. The thread-like forms of *C. pisifera* – 'Filifera' in green, golden 'Filifera Aurea' and the smaller, less thready 'Gold Spangle' – also make good pot plants in their early years. There is also a form of the deodar that makes an attractive container plant with its semi-prostrate growth and golden needle foliage; its name is *Cedrus deodara* 'Golden Horizon'.

BACKDROPS

Green is the pre-eminent colour for the backbone of the garden. It has its own beauty, its own range of tones and textures. The right choice of green can enhance the colours of flowers and 'coloured' (that is, non-green) foliage. In autumn, the bonfire colours of deciduous trees and shrubs are thrown into relief by the greens of conifers. The pale, precious flowers of winter stand out against a dark green background, especially where they catch the low winter sun.

Many of the blue-grey conifers already assigned the status of stars would also perform splendidly as backdrops. They could be joined by others, such as *Juniperus squamata* 'Meyeri', often sold as a dwarf but ultimately reaching 3 m (10 ft), of irregular, spreading habit, with dark blue-glaucous foliage. The forms of *J. × media* 'Pfitzeriana' are also good companions to almost everything, with their 45°-angled branches forming a wide vase-shaped outline, plain green in the type, suffused with yellow in 'Pfitzeriana Aurea' and touched with blue tints in 'Pfitzeriana Glauca'. To introduce a deeper note, you could add *Osmanthus heterophyllus* 'Purpureus', which is more of a purplish green than a true purple, except in its new growths, but is all the more suitable as a quiet backdrop as a result of its colour.

Silver and grey foliage – gleaming and brilliant under the summer sun, and transformed to gentle luminescence by the dews of autumn – is often bedraggled in winter. True year-round greys are not that common, but *Elaeagnus macrophylla* almost qualifies: its large, rounded leaves are silvery when young but pewter green on the upper surface as they mature. In mild regions *Olearia macrodonta* is an attractive steely grey all year, its leaves shaped like holly, though lacking the fierce spines of holly.

In warmer places still – it will withstand only a few degrees of frost – the feijoa, *Acca sellowiana*, develops in time into a big thundercloud of a bush with dark grey-green leaves, white on the reverse to make the silver lining due to any self-respecting cloud. Though it is variegated rather than silver, *Rhamnus alaternus* 'Argenteovariegata' looks platinum-pale from a little distance, its neat, oval leaves marbled with grey and margined white; it forms the perfect, understated backdrop and is hardy too.

The laurustinus, *Viburnum tinus*, is valued for its winter flowers even though they are scentless. The green-leaved form slowly makes a great, cumulus pile of dark, evergreen foliage, rather sombre until it flowers. It has an appealing form, 'Variegatum', with ivory-cream margins to the leaves, too understated for stardom but a pleasant, unfussy backdrop.

TAPESTRIES AND CARPETS

Carpets of plants in the garden, like carpets in the house, can be restful or fussy. Restful need not imply colourless or dull; the distinction is between broad sweeps of a single element or lots of bitty plantings in ones and twos. Let your star turns be in ones and twos by all means – what nursery catalogues are apt to call 'specimen plants'. The brighter and more eye-catching they are, the more they call for a unifying ground planting, be it green or some other colour. Added interest comes from the varying textures and heights of the plants you choose: not just flat carpeters, but hummocks and mounds and domes.

Heathers

Heathers, with or without prostrate and spreading conifers, are widely used to make tapestries and carpets of year-round colour. If used in sufficient masses, they impose their own unity on the garden, despite the range of colours available, which few of us can resist. Even if you add tree heaths and specimen conifers, the basic theme is one of hummocky outlines and tiny leaves.

Most European species of heath have produced scores of varieties, some chosen for flower colour and many for foliage. If you want to use heathers as a quiet, unifying expanse in the garden, cultivars with green or grey foliage are the ones to choose. One of the best greys is *Erica tetralix* 'Alba Mollis', with white flowers in summer, while *Calluna vulgaris* 'Silver Queen' is silvery grey, with soft-mauve flowers in late summer. 'Silver Knight' is similar but slightly taller.

Heaths come not just in grey and silver, but also in lime and gold, orange and flame, coppery maroon and even – in winter, at least – red. Some of the best, in each colour, are listed in the Appendices, under *Calluna* and *Erica*. One of the purest of yellows is that of *Erica vagans* 'Valerie Proudley', a compact little plant.

Many are so bright that they can be hard to position, especially when you consider that their yellow, orange and red foliage might have been designed to clash with the usual heather-flower colours of pinky mauve or purple. *Calluna vulgaris* 'Robert Chapman' looks good in summer with *Erica carnea* 'Vivellii', the first old gold touched with flame, the second bronzed green. Come winter and 'Robert Chapman' is bright orange-red while 'Vivellii' is decked in deep carmine flowers – a mixture which, even in the cold, is painful to the eye. A grey or silver heath would be cooler in summer and more effective at pointing up the winter contrast of grey and red, ashes and embers.

For height without a change of texture, include a specimen, or a group, of tree-heath in one of the coloured forms now on offer. The Mediterranean *Erica erigena* 'Golden Lady' hardly breaks the surface of a sea of heaths but *E. arborea* 'Albert's Gold' really grows upwards, looking like a cluster of narrow, golden-green candle-flames reaching for the sky.

Varying the textures and tints

Many low evergreens make hummocks that can be combined for year-round texture and colour. A group leaning towards yellow and green, for example, might consist of *Phlomis chrysophylla*, a wide dome of broad, yellow-grey, felted leaves; the tight domes of *Santolina rosmarinifolia* var. *rosmarinifolia* (better known as *S. virens*), which, unlike the usual silvery cotton lavenders, is bright, rich green all year; *Ozothamnus ledifolius*, a wide and bumpy hummock of tiny, olive-green, yellow-backed leaves; *Hebe rakaiensis* (syn. *H. subalpina*) in apple green; and the choppy carpet of fresh green of *Juniperus conferta* or the similar *J. taxifolia lutchuensis*, or the rather taller *J.* × *media* 'Mint Julep'.

Emphasizing the yellows

For more emphasis on the yellow tones rather than green, there are several forms of *Juniperus* × *media* with lacy or feathery-looking, yellow-golden foliage (but prickly to the touch, like almost all junipers). Most grow in semi-horizontal fashion, reaching about 90 cm (3 ft) in height and more in width. 'Old Gold', as its name suggests, is yellow touched with bronze; the rather flatter 'Gold Coast' is bright yellow and 'Sulphur Spray' is pale yellow. As well as the growing band of junipers both penny-plain and twopenny-coloured, there is a fine, spreading golden yew, *Taxus baccata* 'Summergold', with bright yellow needles. Another yew that grows sideways rather than up, *T. baccata* 'Repens Aurea', gives the impression of being golden; the broad needles are margined in creamy yellow. *T. baccata* 'Semperaurea' is a yew of semi-erect habit, growing to 1.2 m (4 ft) or so, with broad, golden-yellow needles.

Silver and blue

In a silver and blue-grey group the more familiar cotton lavenders, bobbly silver *Santolina chamaecyparissus* and the feathery *S. pinnata* ssp. *neapolitana*, could be joined by some of the little hebes with grey or glaucous foliage. As well as *Hebe pinguifolia* 'Pagei', one of the flattest in growth, there are the bun-shaped *H. carnosula*, with small, glaucous-grey, shell-shaped leaves, *H. albicans*, *H. colensoi* 'Glauca' and *H.* 'Pewter Dome'. *H. pimeleoïdes* 'Quicksilver' is bluer, with a more spraying, open habit. The odd one out among small hebes is *H. cupressoïdes*, which looks and smells more like a blue-grey conifer than a shrubby veronica; it grows to about 90 cm (3 ft) and there is a compact version of it called 'Boughton Dome'. Though no-one grows border pinks for their foliage alone, most of them have attractive blue-grey or grey-green leaves that add another distinctive note.

Brachyglottis (syn. *Senecio*) *monroi* is a hummocky mound of small, grey-felted leaves with crinkled, white margins, handsome all year, even in winter when the frost picks out each individual leaf with a rim of crystals. If you garden on acid soil you should succeed with the small-leaved rhododendrons that originate from high Himalayan pastures and prefer to be grown in more open positions than their larger cousins. *R. impeditum* would fit well in this scheme, especially in the selection known as 'Blue Steel', and so would the slightly larger-leaved, intensely verdigris-blue *R. lepidostylum*.

Although it grows wide in time, *Juniperus virginiana* 'Grey Owl' is one I would always want to include for its spreading, spraying habit and grey-blue foliage. Keep it well apart from the small, slow-growing rhododendrons, though. It is not so flat as the forms of *J. horizontalis*, of which several are blue-grey or blue-green in colour; 'Bar Harbor', 'Blue Chip', 'Hughes' and 'Wiltonii' are some of the best. Some of the Asiatic junipers also come in bluish shades, among them *J. squamata* 'Blue Carpet'. For a habit that more recalls a starburst than a carpet, there is *J. squamata* 'Blue Star'.

There is also a juniper to link the silver and the golden groups: *J. × media* 'Blue and Gold', with the usual semi-prostrate habit and feathery aspect, and foliage basically blue-grey with splashes of pale gold. A different type of variegation occurs in *Sequoia sempervirens* 'Adpressa', which has cream-tipped shoots. It has a bothersome habit of forsaking its desirable semi-prostrate growth to send a single shoot suddenly aiming for the sky; ruthlessly cut these upwardly mobile shoots out at the base to retain the wide mound which best shows off the pretty colouring.

Purple tones

If you want to add notes of purple, the same caveat applies to the smaller, hummocky plants as to the larger; there are not many evergreen, purple-leaved plants to choose from that look good all year, unless you live in a frost-free area. If the winters in your area are not too severe, you should get away with *Hebe* 'Mrs Winder', a low, rounded evergreen with narrow, bronze-purple leaves, at their darkest in winter. Another smallish shrub is *Pittosporum tenuifolium* 'Tom Thumb', which has very dark, metallic-purple foliage.

Carpets of variegations

A carpet of a single type of variegated plant, used in quantity, need not look fussy, but if you were to mix several of different textures and colours it certainly would. The trouble is that there is quite a choice of variegated euonymuses, ivies and periwinkles, almost all of which are excellent at making an evergreen carpet among taller shrubs. The creeping *Euonymus fortunei* comes in more or less trailing or shrubby variants, and their habit of growth also depends on where you plant them: on the flat, the trailers will spread as a carpet, more or less prostrate according to their nature; but against a wall they turn into climbers and can reach 3 m (10 ft) or more. They will also weave their way into the lower branches of neighbouring shrubs. If these neighbours are deciduous, you have the opportunity of creating some stunning seasonal effects against the evergreen background of the euonymus. The white-variegated 'Silver Queen', which is actually creamy primrose and green in spring, is the perfect foil for the summer garb and bright, autumn tints of purple *Berberis thunbergii*. 'Emerald Gaiety' is white and green, best in quantity when it does indeed look cheerfully pale green, and 'Variegatus' has smaller, white-margined leaves and more decidedly trailing stems. If purple with gold is more to your taste, substitute *Euonymus fortunei* 'Sheridan Gold', cloudy yellow in leaf with green older foliage, or the bright

In spring the nodding, lily-like flowers of Erythronium *'White Beauty' find a perfect backdrop in the white-variegated* Euonymus fortunei *'Variegatus'.*

'Emerald 'n' Gold', which takes on pink tints in winter in full exposure, or 'Sunspot'.

The variegated forms of *Vinca minor*, the lesser periwinkle, range from white to yellow, all of them reasonably effective in the mass, though none so showy as the variegated greater periwinkle, *V. major*. This can look quite stunning even in the most unlikely situations, as, for example, planted at the base of a clipped thorn hedge, where in winter its bold ivory and green leaves on scrambling stems pop up here and there among the dark, leafless mass of the hedge. Although the greater periwinkle is not just larger in leaf but also much more vigorous than the lesser, it is *V. minor* which makes the better carpet. It comes in both white- and yellow-variegated forms.

As for ivies, forms of *Hedera helix*, there are so many named kinds that the best advice may be to go to your local nursery or garden centre and buy the one you like best. Of the variegated forms, I would choose from: 'Goldheart' with its neat, triangular leaves centrally splashed with canary yellow; the cloudy-yellow 'Angularis Aurea'; and the small-leaved 'Buttercup', as bright as its name suggests if you find the right place for it, not too dry lest it scorch, nor too shady lest it turn green. White-variegated ivies include 'Glacier', very understated in ivory on grey; tiny-leaved 'Adam' which is rather too open in growth to make a good cover; 'Luzii' with leaves heavily flecked cream to give an overall greyish effect; and 'Little Diamond', which really belongs in a hanging basket on account of the way its stems all radiate out from the centre. On the flat it looks a bit like a variegated starfish, but a very leafy one.

Swathes of grassy-leaved plants

The narrow leaves of grasses – from threads to swords, but nothing broader – and their graceful movement are the ideal counterpoint to the heavier masses of broad-leaved plants, and their essentially vertical outlines give a lift to rounded and horizontal lines, while the repetition of identical blades in a wide sweep adds coherence and unity. Of similar aspect to the true grasses are the sedges and plants such as the lily turfs. Among the smaller, grassy-leaved plants are some that are evergreen, beautiful all year and ideally adapted to spreading in generous swathes. *Carex hachijoensis* (syn. *C. morrowii*) 'Evergold' makes tussocks of narrow, arching blades with a bold stripe of yellow down the centre of each, while *C. morrowii* 'Fisher's Form' is slightly taller and the slender leaves are margined with yellow. Equally bright is *Acorus gramineus* 'Ogon', an aroid with leaves as fine as any grass, with broad, golden margins. (In the USA this is known as 'Oborozuki' while 'Ogon' refers to a different, less vividly variegated cultivar.)

Cream to white variegations belong to another small sedge, *Carex conica* 'Snowline', and to the brilliantly pale lily turf known as *Liriope* 'Silvery Sunproof', which is not so tough and needs shelter as well as shade to grow the finest foliage. *L. muscari* 'John Burch' is variegated in cream and ivory, and is more resistant to both sun and frost. Another hardy lily turf is *L. muscari* 'Gold Banded', with yellow stripes along the leaves.

Black is a rare colour in the garden, though some flowers seem to come near to it, until you hold them next to a piece of black cloth. But there is one plant with really black leaves, forming tufts of narrow blades: *Ophiopogon planiscapus* 'Nigrescens'. It needs the right companions to show at its true value; I fancy it might look well with the chocolate-veined, dark grey leaves of *Heuchera* 'Pewter Moon'.

For a very unusual combination, pair the black ophiopogon with one of the red-leaved sedges. *Uncinia unciniata* and *U. rubra* are the best known; they (or it, for the name *rubra* is often applied to *U. uncinata*) have bright, rust-red to maroon blades. Brighter still, especially in winter, is *U. egmontiana*; in summer it is chocolate and madder brown, in winter rich mahogany red. Just to confuse, it too is sometimes labelled *U. rubra*. *Schoenus pauciflorus* has narrow, upright blades of rich maroon colouring with contrasting green at the base.

CHAPTER 3

THE NEW GROWTHS OF SPRING

ALL LEAVES CHANGE COLOUR from their first unfurling to maturity, but the most exciting spring growths of all are those that are brightly coloured. Even some of the plants we grow mainly for their flowers can contribute to the spring picture with the colours of their unfolding leaves.

There is a spring-bright plant for every garden, whatever its soil; but you do need to remember that new growths, whether tender green or brightly coloured, are more vulnerable than mature foliage to drying or icy winds, late frosts, or even a sudden hot day, and will easily scorch if you do not give them some protection. If the point of growing a plant is its spring foliage, you need to be doubly sure of choosing the right place for it lest you should lose the display to an untimely night of frost or spring heatwave.

PAINTING THE SKY WITH BRIGHT SPRING FOLIAGE

A surprising number of trees, even those that we choose principally for their flowers, have colourful young foliage. Take flowering cherries. Chosen carefully, they have much more to offer than just those flounces of sugar-pink or white blossom. Several add tinted spring foliage as well. The prototype of the Japanese cherries is *Prunus jamasakura* (syn. *P. serrulata* var. *spontanea*), a variable tree which, in its best forms, has rich coppery-red to mahogany young leaves and pure white flowers. These Japanese cherries can become quite bulky but there are some enchanting smaller flowering cherries to be had. 'Pandora' has shell-pink flowers, bronze-red spring foliage and bright autumn tints, and 'Kursar' is rich pink in flower, the last blooms coinciding with the unfurling, red-bronze leaves.

The rowans are generally planted for their autumn colour and berries, and *Sorbus cashmeriana* is no exception. But it has a double bonus – soft-pink flowers instead of the usual off-white and, better still, spring foliage that emerges in tints of crimson, blood red and pink. Like all the rowans, the leaves are divided into many leaflets, while those of the related whitebeams are undivided. A selected form of whitebeam, *S. aria* 'Lutescens', is outstanding in spring when the chalice-

Few trees are as startling in spring as this form of sycamore, Acer pseudoplatanus 'Brilliantissimum'.

like unfolding leaf buds are as soft to the eye and the touch as ivory-white velvet. Later the upper surface deepens to grey-green.

The pride of India or golden rain tree, *Koelreuteria paniculata*, needs hot summers to flower freely. It is worth growing even where it does not flower regularly, because of its spring foliage, tinted at first with pink and bronze. Another Chinese tree with ash-like leaves is *Toona* (syn. *Cedrela*) *sinensis*, of which the cultivar aptly known as 'Flamingo' is bright coral red and pink in its spring garb. Both the Chinese toon and the pride of India turn golden in autumn.

Maples are renowned for their autumn colour above all, yet some start their display in spring. The one that almost everyone knows is a form of sycamore, *Acer pseudoplatanus* 'Brilliantissimum'. Very slow-growing but definitely a tree rather than a shrub, this has leaves of typical sycamore shape but very untypical colouring in spring; the new growths are bright shrimp pink and coral, fading through apricot to cream and never really making it back to a wholehearted green. The same is not true of 'Prinz Handjery', almost identical in spring but maturing in summer to a healthy green with soft-purple reverse. It is now almost as widely available as 'Brilliantissimum', and in my view, is a much better garden plant. Another maple that runs to vivid spring tints is *A. cappadocicum*; the form 'Aureum' unfurls in shades of red before passing to clear yellow for the rest of the season, while 'Rubrum' is blood red at first, passing to green.

Last but not least among trees that paint the spring sky with colour is *Aesculus neglecta* 'Erythroblastos', a horse chestnut that slowly grows to small-tree stature, its palmate leaves unfurling like tiny, fragile fingers in shades of coral, scarlet and pink, and fading as they expand to soft chartreuse green.

BENEATH THE CANOPY

Below the spreading branches of your trees, or even in the shelter of a single tree, you can begin to create an idealized woodland in miniature. The smaller ornamental trees are far better for this purpose than large, light-excluding and root-greedy trees such as beech or holm oak. Many of the shrubs that we grow for their vivid spring foliage are at their best in dappled shade, sheltered from the cold winds or sudden sunny days that could scorch their tender new leaves and spoil the season's display. Their companions will be lacy ferns unscrolling from crozier-like buds, and the shell-case snouts of hostas, later unfolding into broad blades. With them we can grow epimediums and dicentras and, for contrast of outline, shade-loving grasses such as lemon-gold *Milium effusum* 'Aureum'.

For lime-free soil only

Some of the finest shade-loving shrubs chosen for their brilliant spring foliage are resolutely calcifuge, that is, they will not grow where there is lime in the soil. If this is your case, you will have to resort to growing them in containers, or raised beds perhaps, of specially prepared soil and forgo the naturalistic woodland effects.

The brightest display comes from the pierises, a whole range of which have now been selected for brilliance of colour. Best of all are the forms of the *Pieris formosa* var. *forrestii*, which can grow to 1.8 m (6 ft) or more. The new leaves are a pure and vivid scarlet against the previous season's deep green foliage, slowly passing through coral pink, primrose yellow, pale green and then the dark green of maturity, with often a second flush later in the season. These tender young growths are all too easily burned by an untimely spring frost; the overhead canopy of a tree will help to protect them, but you should also choose a position away from icy winds.

A long-established selection of this wonderful shrub is *Pieris formosa* var. *forrestii* 'Wakehurst'. 'Charles Michael' is another scarlet stunner, with larger than normal, white, lily-of-the-valley like flowers. 'Jermyns', in grenadier scarlet, also has bold, showy sprays of flowers. There are two first-rate hybrids, evocatively named 'Forest Flame' and 'Firecrest', both a little shorter in growth but just as colourful. 'Bert Chandler' can be red or butter yellow in young leaf.

Many forms of *Pieris japonica* have been chosen for their flowers, which come in pink or claret as well as white, rather than for their more muted, coppery-bronzed new growths. But some of the newer kinds emulate the *formosa* types, leaning towards scarlet and crimson: 'Purity' in red-bronze, 'Scarlett O'Hara' in red, 'Tilford' in crimson-scarlet, and the long-lasting 'Mountain Fire'. 'Flaming Silver' starts out bright red and matures to green edged with white.

You need plenty of fresh green around your pierises. Then the coppery red of *Rhododendron lutescens*, a tall, open shrub with pointed leaves and primrose-lemon flowers, or the chocolate brown of *R. williamsianum*, which has almost circular leaves and makes a low mound, will not be overshadowed by the brilliance of the pierises. 'Bow Bells' and 'Winsome' are pretty hybrids with the blood of *R. williamsianum* and also something of its spring leaf colour, copper and bronze. In contrast, the ever popular *R. yakushimanum*, with its tight, rounded habit, prim trusses of pink and white flowers, and narrow, neat leaves, is silver-felted in spring. *R. cinnabarinum* is different again, with its oval, glaucous leaves, intensely blue as they unfurl, the perfect setting for the ochre-yellow bells.

Most hardy hybrid rhododendrons, that group of big shrubs with large trusses of flowers that you can grow right in the open, have very boring leaves. But 'Moser's Maroon' is an exception; it does indeed have maroon flowers, but best of all its young growths are rich maroon-purple.

The neat, small leaves of vacciniums make their effect by the pattern they form on the spraying branches. Some of the evergreen species are quietly colourful in new growth. From the smallest to the largest, you could choose from *V.*

Only for acid soils – but where it thrives, Pieris *'Forest Flame' is as bright as any flower in its scarlet spring livery. The sprays of white, urn-shaped flowers are a pretty bonus.*

moupinense, at 30 cm (12 in), with golden-brown spring foliage; *V. floribundum*, 90 cm (3 ft), with mahogany-red young leaves; or *V. ovatum*, 1.8 m (6 ft), its new foliage coppery mahogany. *Leucothoë* 'Scarletta' is a recent introduction which has the typical pointed leaves of its tribe but, unlike others, is almost as bright red as a pieris in spring and summer.

You will need lime-free soil, too, for the Chinese tupelo, *Nyssa sinensis*, a large shrub or small tree with bright red young growths all spring and summer; after a short spell of greenery, it lights up again in autumn.

Most people grow camellias for their sumptuous flowers but, if you have an eye for foliage, you will appreciate *Camellia cuspidata*. Its flowers are simple, white and small, and its leaves are at first copper to mahogany black, with a high gloss finish. With that, we are almost done with the lime-haters, but no foliage addict with suitable soil would want to be without a recent introduction, the deciduous *Fothergilla gardenii* 'Blue Mist', which bears rounded leaves of a unique almost powder blue in spring, passing to blue-green as the season advances.

Shrubs for cool, woodsy soil

Most corylopsises will stand a little lime, but *Corylopsis pauciflora* is better in acid soil. A smallish shrub, it has cowslip-scented, primrose-yellow bells on bare branches in early spring and a bonus of coral and pink new growths. Keep it out of the way of cold wind and frost, which burn the tender young leaves. Some people say the witch hazels are lime-haters too, but I believe they need a leafy, cool soil rather than a specifically acid one and hate to dry out in summer. The gem of the witch hazels in spring is *Hamamelis vernalis* 'Sandra', which has plum-purple young foliage. To contrast with its broad, rounded leaves, you could plant a fern, *Dryopteris erythrosora*, which has typically lacy fronds, except that they unfurl in shades of copper and pink before turning to pale fresh green.

The same conditions suit *Corylopsis willmottiae* 'Spring Purple', a name that says it all, except that, like all its tribe, it has fragrant, lemon flowers, in little sprays, as well as smoky-purple spring foliage. At its feet you could grow epimediums. Their daintily divided young leaves also show a range of subtle colours, from purple to bronze, copper and something very near pink. Epimediums are best planted in shade but, once established, will happily spread into the sun and come to no harm. They look their best among shrubs; another fitting companion would be *Viburnum sargentii* 'Onandago', with its plum-purple young foliage.

The Japanese maples, *Acer palmatum*, are always best away from chill winds and with their roots in a fluffy, leafy soil that does not dry out. Many are bright in spring, a bonus for a plant we grow above all for its autumn effect, and one of the best is also among the brightest at leaf fall: 'Osakazuki', scarlet in young foliage. 'Shindeshojo' and 'Shishio' are also scarlet; 'Corallinum' is coral pink, and 'Katsura' is an appealing combination of orange-buff and red.

OUT IN THE SUN

You can also have bright spring foliage in the sunnier parts of your garden. The evergreen photinias will not only stand an open site, but several are also as bright

Fig 4 *In autumn, all Japanese maples (forms of* Acer palmatum*) are so bright they seem to be lit by their own internal fires; with its incandescent scarlet and crimson tones, 'Osakazuki' is outstanding.*

as a pieris, yet have no dislike of lime. The ones to look for are the *Photinia × fraseri* group, with descriptive names such as 'Red Robin' and 'Redstart', and the older 'Rubens'. Do not despise 'Robusta' or 'Birmingham' because their names are boring; their spring foliage is not dull in the least. The new growth of all these is bright scarlet with a hint of copper, slowly passing to deep green.

The sacred bamboo, *Nandina domestica* – which isn't a bamboo at all – is often planted by the Japanese by their doorways. Whatever magical properties they attribute to it, one thing is certain: it is highly decorative all year round, with its unbranched stems and large, evergreen, divided leaves, often coloured in shades of coral and terracotta to scarlet in spring and again in autumn. There is a dwarf form, 'Pygmaea', and one well-named 'Firepower'.

Fig 5 *The Japanese call* Nandina domestica *the sacred bamboo, and grow it by the doors of their houses, where they can see it change through the seasons as they confide in it their dreams and hopes.*

Conifers for spring tints

Almost all conifers are best in an open, sunny place and those that have bright spring foliage are no exception. Most of them go in for golden or creamy-yellow tints, which accord so well with the fresh greens and sharp yellows of the spring scene but need to be kept away from pink cherries and crabs. For these, whether or not they have coloured spring foliage, the taller blue-grey conifers are ideal companions. One that is especially fresh and pale in spring is *Chamaecyparis lawsoniana* 'Silver Queen', its new growths silvery cream against the flat sprays of the mature, grey-green foliage. 'White Spot' and the Ellwoodii sport, 'Snow White', also show off their white variegations to best effect in the spring.

Set off by the black-green, glossy foliage of *Prunus laurocerasus* 'Otto Luyken' or *Phillyrea latifolia*, golden conifers are at their best. 'Otto Luyken' has a stiffly upright, though broad, outline, and I like to contrast it with a near-prostrate conifer such as *Juniperus communis* 'Depressa Aurea', the branches of which spread low and wide, drooping at the tips, which in spring are butter yellow against the coppery-bronze winter tints of the previous season's foliage. In summer it ripens to old gold. Flatter than this, and paler creamy gold, is *J. squamata* 'Holger'. If you want a narrow column to form the third element in the composition, it might be *J. chinensis* 'Aurea', its new growths silvery gold against the yellow of the previous season and deeper gold of the oldest foliage.

The compact, formal cone of *Picea orientalis* 'Aurea' calls for low-growing companions that will not crowd it and, ideally, a backdrop of dark green. Against this, its creamy-yellow new shoots, which deepen to gold and then green, are given full value. A newer version of this, slower and more compact in growth and, if possible, even brighter in spring, is known as 'Wittboldt'. Both have more appeal, to my eye at least, than the golden Christmas tree, *P. abies* 'Aurea', with its year-round colouring of off-yellow against which the brighter spring growths hardly show up. If you prefer the romantically irregular silhouette of the Scots pine, its golden form (*Pinus sylvestris* 'Aurea') is very bright in spring.

WAKING UP THE FLOWER BORDER WITH SPRING FOLIAGE

Most flower borders are at their best in summer and there is a lot to be said for a concentrated effort on one season. But, in small gardens, a one-shot border is a luxury: all that colour for a few short weeks may mean going without for nine months of the year. One way around the problem is to include plenty of perennials, and perhaps some shrubs, with colourful spring foliage. Happily, many of them have beautiful flowers as well.

Take day lilies, a mainstay of the summer border. They all have sword-shaped leaves and some are a bright but tender shade of chartreuse yellow when first emerging in spring. Among the best are the old tawny day lily, *Hemerocallis fulva*, in both elegant single-flowered and longer-lasting double forms; and the sweetly scented lemon lily, *H. lilioasphodelus* (syn. *H. flava*). Both increase freely at the root and grow equally well in sun or light shade. To emphasize the yellow theme in a shady border, there are two stalwart old hostas, *Hosta fortunei* var. *albopicta,* with broad, butter-yellow leaves edged with pale jade green, and the all-yellow *H. f. aurea*, pale and lovely in spring. Both fade to a soft uniform green, with just the shadow of variegation in the first, in summer. Also for shade is *Geranium* × *monacense* 'Muldoon' (syn. *G. punctatum*); its lobed leaves in spring are pale yellow, against which the dark maroon spots at the base of each lobe stand out clearly; later the primrose colouring matures to soft green. The spring colouring of *Valeriana phu* 'Aurea' is brighter, an eye-catching, slightly sharp yellow; its drawbacks are summer leafage of the most boring green and its irresistible attraction for cats, which chew it to shreds.

For something altogether more aristocratic, even if it too turns largely green in summer, choose *Astrantia major* 'Sunningdale Variegated', with divided leaves boldly splashed with creamy yellow. It is best in sun and can be set in a carpet of the purple-leaved *Viola riviniana* 'Purpurea' (syn. *V. labradorica*) or the more metallic, bronzed purple of the bugle, *Ajuga reptans* 'Atropurpurea'. A different change of colour occurs in *Stachys byzantina* 'Primrose Heron', a form of lamb's ears with velvety-soft leaves that start life in spring in shades of chartreuse and

Hosta fortunei *var.* albopicta *is at its most appealing in spring, when the broad blades are still brightly splashed with primrose yellow. Here it makes a cool harmony with Mr Bowles's golden grass,* Milium effusum *'Aureum', and a yellow globe flower (*Trollius*).*

butter yellow before reverting in summer to the more familiar bright silver.

Most variegated plants, happily, do not turn green as summer advances but it is a characteristic of several yellow or cream variegations to fade towards ivory or white. Where there are two forms of a plant, one yellow-variegated and one white-variegated, they will be at their most distinct in spring and may be impossible to tell apart after midsummer.

Other variegated plants retain their basic green and cream, or green and yellow, but are touched in spring with pink or coral. Such is the grass *Glyceria maxima* var. *variegata*, the cream-striped blades of which are distinctly pink at first. It does well in moist soil, or even in shallow water, but runs less at the root, and develops brighter colours, in drier soil.

The contrast between fresh, pale tones and the rich crimsons and mahogany reds of young paeony shoots is as bright as any floral display. These are the Chinese paeonies derived from *Paeonia lactiflora*, all of them with sumptuous flowers to follow their spring outburst. More subtle are the dove-grey and pink spring tints of *P. mlokosewitschii*, or the grey-green and copper of *P. obovata* var. *alba*, two exquisite, single-flowered paeonies. Behind such a group you might set the beauty bush, *Kolkwitzia amabilis*, which has not only enchanting flowers like small, peach-pink foxgloves, but also young foliage of a pretty shade of buff pink.

Another way to treat the richer tones is to emphasize them with deep red and near-black tulips. *Heuchera americana* is a fitting element in such a grouping, with its satin-finished, ivy-shaped leaves, flushed and veined with copper and mahogany when young. Give it good living and it will keep on producing new leaves well into the summer. The milk-chocolate tones of *Lysimachia ciliata* are at their most emphatic in spring, later fading to pale copper. In full sun, *Oenothera fruticosa* precedes its summer display of yellow suncups with rich mahogany-red spring foliage. The spiraeas with coppery-gold foliage, forms of *Spiraea japonica*, are good, mixed-border shrubs, small and twiggy, essentially formless and suitable for hard pruning to ensure fresh, vivid leaves. The basic foliage colour of 'Goldflame', 'Gold Mound' and 'Golden Princess' is lime yellow, but, especially in spring, they are flushed and tipped with bright copper and orange-pink.

If your soil is consistently damp, you should succeed with astilbes. Before their plumy and feathery flowers open, the spring foliage, especially of those with deeper pink and red colouring, is richly tinted and as crisply divided as a fern but of crimson, mahogany and copper tones that no fern ever boasted. Among smaller cultivars are 'Bronze Elegance' and 'Dunkellachs', both with coppery foliage. For a strong contrast of both colour and form, pair the larger, mahogany-leaved astilbes with *Iris pseudacorus* 'Variegata', a form of the yellow flag with its sword leaves brightly striped in creamy yellow until its midsummer flowering season, when they fade to mid-green. Cut off the seed heads before they ripen or you will have a mass of plain green seedlings. If you decide to risk the grass *Glyceria maxima* var. *variegata* in a moist place, it too makes a pretty companion for astilbes.

Opposite: *In spring the garden wakes in white, with 'Mount Tacoma' tulips and the white-bordered blades of* Hosta crispula.

Fig 6 *Not quite so massive as gunnera, the ornamental rhubarb,* Rheum palmatum *'Atrosanguineum', has rich crimson and blood-red colouring which is revealed as the great leaves unfurl and retained throughout the summer on the leaf backs.*

Damp soil also suits *Euphorbia sikkimensis*, a tall spurge with the usual greeny-yellow flowers in summer, preceded by new shoots in early spring of translucent ruby red and scarlet. For sheer magnificence, the ornamental rhubarb, *Rheum palmatum* 'Atrosanguineum', is at its best in spring when the great, jaggedly lobed leaves unfurl in rich crimson, maturing to dark green with the crimson tints retained on the reverse of the leaf. The moisture-loving sensitive fern, *Onoclea sensibilis*, with its fingered leaves of fresh lettuce green, is an ideal partner. It will grow even with its feet in water, whereas the rheum needs a moist but drained soil; it will rot if kept too wet.

CHAPTER 4

SUMMER LEAVES

A S SPRING SETTLES INTO SUMMER, foliage is more than ever dominant. Beneath the leafy canopy, hostas and dicentras reach their full summer perfection. Out in the sun, the silvers that winter left bedraggled are once again platinum pale. In damp places, there is a veritable jungle of lush foliage. And borders and containers are bursting with energy and colour; it is up to you how much of that is flower colour, and how much belongs to plants with lovely leaves.

THE LEAFY CANOPY

Some of the most beautiful foliage plants, green or coloured, are those that revel in dappled shade. Planting a tree should be a priority; and happily, among the trees to choose from, there are plenty with foliage that is more than just a shady canopy and will itself contribute to the colourful picture.

Silver and gold overhead

As the sharp greens of spring settle into heavier summer greenery, pale, silver-grey or glaucous foliage overhead adds a cooling touch to the picture. Hardy trees with silver foliage are not many but two of them, though both rather large for the average garden, have an added allure: both the white poplar, *Populus alba*, and the weeping silver lime, *Tilia* 'Petiolaris', have leaves that flutter in the wind to reveal their pale, silvery reverse. The silver willow, *Salix alba* var. *sericea*, is also large in maturity, with narrow leaves shimmering in the breeze like shoals of silver fishes.

To underplant the weeping silver pear, *Pyrus salicifolia* 'Pendula', you will need to train it; for its ambition is to make a low, domed tree with branches weeping to the ground, clad with willow-like, palest grey leaves. The oleaster, *Elaeagnus angustifolia*, looks almost like an olive tree in leaf, with its narrow, silvery-white foliage; but it is a hardy, deciduous shrub or small tree with tiny, pale yellow, fragrant flowers in summer and pale amber fruits.

The golden locust, *Robinia pseudoacacia* 'Frisia', has leaves of bright, insistent yellow. The golden form of the honey locust, *Gleditsia triacanthos* 'Sunburst', is daintier in leaf, though its chartreuse-yellow spring colouring fades in summer to lime green before turning chrome yellow again in autumn. There is also a yellow form of the box elder, *Acer negundo* 'Auratum', though its pinnate leaves are coarse by comparison. The golden rowan, *Sorbus aucuparia* 'Dirkenii', has pinnate leaves typical of rowans, yellow in spring but tarnishing to green as summer advances.

Near where I live someone has planted *Robinia* 'Frisia' with the golden Indian bean tree, *Catalpa bignonioïdes* 'Aurea'. The contrast is stunning in a setting of darker greens, for the catalpa has huge, heart-shaped leaves, of a yellow nearer to lime than the robinia. The leaves of the golden whitebeam, *Sorbus aria* 'Chrysophylla', are also rounded, though smaller; they are yellow-green, with white-felted reverse. The white poplar, too, has a golden form, 'Richardii', in which the yellow upper surface contrasts with the white leaf backs. There is a golden form of the silver birch, too: *Betula pendula* 'Golden Cloud' has leaves that are clear yellow all season. It needs shelter from cold winds and dislikes drought.

I have already extolled *Acer cappadocicum* 'Aureum' because of its red spring growths; it is a handsome yellow-leaved tree for summer also. The golden sycamore, *A. pseudoplatanus* 'Worleei', begins the season in soft lime yellow, deepening to a purer yellow but aging, as summer ripens, to green. Also starting yellow but turning green is the golden beech, *Fagus sylvatica* 'Zlatia'; it is very slow-growing. The golden oak, *Quercus robur* 'Concordia', is also slow to make a tree. Another familiar tree that boasts a golden form is the grey alder; *Alnus incana* 'Aurea' is a delightful, slender tree with small yellow leaves and orange-red winter catkins. The golden hop tree, *Ptelea trifoliata* 'Aurea', hovers between shrub and tree status. It has leaves of soft yellow-green.

Yellow-variegated trees are not many but among them is a real aristocrat, the variegated tulip tree, *Liriodendron tulipifera* 'Aureomarginatum'; its bold, saddle-shaped leaves with their curious, squared-off tips are boldly margined with lime yellow. The variegated sweet gum, *Liquidambar styraciflua* 'Aurea', has leaves striped and splashed with yellow. There are two forms of the variegated sweet chestnut (*Castanea sativa*): 'Albomarginata' ('Argenteovariegata') with ivory-white leaf margins and 'Variegata', formerly named 'Aureomarginata', which aptly described the broad yellow margins to its toothed leaves. Both grow slowly

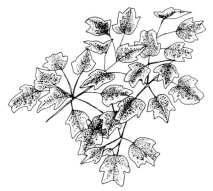

Fig 7 *The tulip tree,* Liriodendron tulipifera, *has leaves as big as a man's hand, with tips that look as if they have been chopped squarely off; in 'Aureomarginatum', shown here, the outline is emphasized by the yellow leaf margins.*

and are apt to revert to green. The variegated Norway maple, *Acer platanoïdes* 'Drummondii', has leaves boldly edged in white. For something of more modest dimensions, there is *Cornus florida* 'Rainbow', with yellow margins. There are two variegated forms of the box elder, too, as well as the all-yellow one. *Acer negundo* 'Elegans' has the usual pinnate leaves, edged with yellow, and 'Variegatum' has white margins. They are good-tempered and easy trees.

Purple, copper and bronze

Trees with purple foliage can be magnificent; think of a mature copper or purple beech. Aficionados without rolling acres can plant *Fagus sylvatica* 'Rohanii', a purple, cut-leaved beech, slower-growing and more restrained, or 'Purpurea Pendula', the weeping purple beech. Though they contribute nothing to the canopy, I cannot omit mention of the fastigiate beeches: 'Dawyck' in plain green and its copper and yellow counterparts, 'Dawyck Purple' and 'Dawyck Gold'. All make narrow columns, very telling in the summer landscape.

Another large tree is the purple Norway maple, *Acer platanoïdes* 'Crimson King'. The more usual choice for small gardens is a purple crab or plum. The plums are selections of *Prunus cerasifera*, the cherry plum: 'Nigra', with dark purple foliage, and 'Pissardii', which unfurls dark red leaves that age to purple; both are a heavy presence in the summer garden. The hybrid of 'Pissardii', known as *P.* × *blireana*, is more of a large shrub than a tree, with metallic-purple foliage. The crabs include 'Aldenhamensis', 'Eleyi' and 'Lemoinei'; they start out purple but turn to bronze-green. 'Royalty' is more intense in red-purple.

There are far more aristocratic purple-leaved trees than these, ranging from a birch, *Betula pendula* 'Purpurea', with small, dark metallic-purple leaves and the usual white bark, to a bean tree, *Catalpa* × *erubescens* 'Purpurea', with very large, very dark purple leaves fading to deep green. There is a form of the Canadian redbud, *Cercis canadensis*, called 'Forest Pansy', an appealing tree with rich purple, rounded leaves; and a charmer of a honey locust, *Gleditsia triacanthos* 'Rubylace', as pretty as its name with dainty fronds, red-purple aging to bronzed green.

Trees of many colours

Trees with multi-coloured foliage can be hard to place. Most of them have pink and white variegations, which will effectively rule out any plant in the yellow, orange or scarlet range of the spectrum.

The box elder that everyone falls for nowadays is *Acer negundo* 'Flamingo', with its pink spring foliage maturing to pink, white and green. There is a beech, not too huge in maturity, *Fagus sylvatica* 'Purpurea Tricolor', that is basically a purple beech but with each leaf rimmed in pale pink; it is rather unstable and apt to turn into an all-purple beech. The variegated thorn, *Crataegus laevigata* 'Gireoudii', with leaves mottled cream and pink, is slow-growing and hardly canopy material but quite pretty. *Cornus florida* 'Welchii' ('Tricolor') is also perhaps more of a middle-storey than a canopy tree and attractive with its white-edged, rose-flushed leaves. As for the sycamore that rejoices in the name of 'Leopoldii' – well, some people evidently like green leaves stained with yellowish pink and purple.

SPRING-FRESH IN SUMMER –
FOLIAGE IN THE SHADE

First come the shrubs and small trees that need dappled shade and shelter from wind, and pre-eminent among these are the Japanese maples. The main distinction is between those with leaves of the standard Japanese maple shape – sharply five- or seven-lobed – and the Dissectum group, with each lobe further dissected until the whole leaf is as fine as lace. The basic leaf colour is bright green, but there are several with purple foliage, known as the *Acer palmatum* Atropurpureum group if seed-raised or, if cut-leaved, as the Dissectum Atropurpureum group; among the best named kinds are black-maroon 'Bloodgood', 'Crimson Queen' and the lacy 'Dissectum Nigrum', 'Burgundy Lace', 'Garnet' and 'Inaba-shidare'.

There are variegated Japanese maples, too: 'Butterfly' with white-margined, pink-touched leaves; 'Asahi-zuru' in green, pink and white; 'Dissectum Variegatum', which is purple-margined, rose and cream; 'Kagiri-nishiki' ('Roseomarginatum'), pale green edged with coral pink, unstable and apt to revert; and 'Higasayamo', green edged with cream and margined rose pink.

Japanese maples with yellow foliage are few, though you can have both plain and cut-leaved forms by choosing 'Aureum' and 'Dissectum Flavescens', though the latter is hardly more than pale green. They are outshone by the beautiful form of the Japanese full moon maple, *Acer shirasawanum* f. *aureum* (syn. *A. japonicum* f. *aureum)* with its leaves of rounded, lobed outline. Grown with a modicum of shade to keep it from scorching, it will all too slowly make a small, many-stemmed tree with clear yellow foliage.

Most white-variegated shrubs, especially if they are deciduous, also need some shade to develop their best variegations and avoid scorch. There is a rather striking variegated hydrangea, *Hydrangea macrophylla* 'Tricolor', with cream, yellow and grey variegations on pale green. Other white-variegated shrubs will be discussed later in this section, for they perform an essential role in linking shade plantings to those of the flower border.

The leafy carpet

Many of the loveliest leaves belong to perennials that thrive in the filtered light beneath an open tree canopy. The variety in leaf shape is great, from the lacy fronds of ferns to the rapiers of grasses and the broad or near-circular leaves of hostas. One fern, above all, stands out: the Japanese painted fern, *Athyrium niponicum* var. *pictum*, its fronds glaucous grey touched with crimson, on maroon stems. Dissected leaves of the kind often described as 'ferny' belong to the dicentras, several of which are bluish in leaf, such as *Dicentra* 'Langtrees' or the very finely cut *D. formosa* 'Stuart Boothman', with deep pink lockets against steel-blue foliage. They can be matched with the bluer hostas, ranging from *H.*

Opposite: *The Golden full-moon maple,* Acer shirasawanum *f.* aureum, *is slow to make a tree, but even in youth it has great presence thanks to its fresh chartreuse-yellow colouring.*

Fig 8 Hosta *'Krossa Regal'*, *unlike most other large hostas, has an unusual, upstanding habit the better to display the white reverse of its blue-grey leaves.*

sieboldiana var. *elegans* with its great, corrugated dinner-plates, intensely blue 'Big Daddy' with puckered leaves, or the upstanding, pale grey-blue, white-backed 'Krossa Regal', to the many selections of *H.* × *tardiana* with names such as 'Buckshaw Blue', 'Hadspen Blue', 'Blue Moon', 'Blue Wedgwood' and 'Halcyon'. *H. tokudama* resembles a half-sized *sieboldiana* var. *elegans*, with cupped, deeply ribbed, blue-bloomy leaves. Remember, if you are planning a shady area with a range of hostas, that the blues will take more sun than those with variegated leaves.

Most grey-leaved plants need sun and sharp drainage but do not believe pundits who tell you all of them do. Several lungworts are as bright as platinum because of the silver blotches that cover part or all of their broad leaves; look for *Pulmonaria saccharata* 'Argentea' or *P. vallarsae* 'Margery Fish'. At a lower level, the badger-faced *Lamium maculatum* has given rise to several silver-leaved forms, 'Beacon Silver' and 'Red Nancy' with magenta flowers, 'White Nancy' with white. The yellow-flowered *L. galeobdolen* is hopelessly rampageous, but its silver-netted forms, 'Silberteppich' and 'Hermann's Pride', are more restrained.

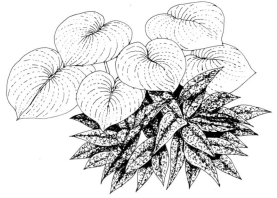

Fig 9 *As big as dinner plates, the leaves of* Hosta sieboldiana *var.* elegans *contrast strikingly with the narrow, silver-blotched blades of* Pulmonaria longifolia.

Gilded leaves

Gold, not silver, is the colour of several superb hostas, which unlike the old *Hosta fortunei aurea* keep their colouring throughout the season. I have space to mention only a few. One of the largest is 'Sum and Substance', with rounded, lime-yellow leaves; 'Zounds', with noticeably ribbed leaves, is another big one. 'Piedmont Gold' is a size smaller and, among the really small ones are 'Hydon Sunset', 'Golden Prayers' and narrow-leaved 'Wogon'. The meadowsweet, *Filipendula ulmaria* 'Aurea', contrasts sharply cut foliage with the hostas; it is a fresh lime yellow in ideal conditions of light shade and a moist soil. The soft blades of Mr Bowles's golden grass, *Milium effusum* 'Aureum', add another outline. To scuttle about the feet of such a golden planting you could tuck in the golden creeping Jenny, *Lysimachia nummularia* 'Aurea', the pick-a-back plant, *Tolmeia menziesii* 'Taff's Gold', or the helxine, *Soleirolia soleirolii* 'Aurea', a mere film of yellow over damp soil.

Variegated hostas

There are plenty of first-rate variegated hostas – every size from dinner-plate to blades hardly bigger than your thumb. The big ones are *Hosta sieboldiana* 'Frances Williams', basically *elegans* with a bold yellow margin, and the forms of *H. ventricosa*: var. *aureomaculata* with a yellow central splash, and 'Aureomarginata' which is, of course, yellow-edged. *H. fortunei* var. *aureomarginata* (also known as 'Obscura Marginata') is almost as bold. The very blue *H. tokudama* has two variegated forms: *flavocircinalis* with yellow margins; and *aureonebulosa* which is hazed yellow.

Among the newer kinds are 'Wide Brim', its broad, blue-green leaves margined with yellow, and 'Gold Standard', in which the leaves are yellow with a rich green margin. 'Shade Fanfare' is green with a creamy-yellow margin. Of similar size is 'Francee', in green edged with white. All these are excellent in containers. The most famous of white-margined hostas is 'Thomas Hogg', now known as *H. undulata* var. *albomarginata*; *H. crispula* is another, distinguished by the long tip to the leaves. *H. fortunei* 'Albomarginata' is also white-edged; keep it clear of overhanging branches because, like the *sieboldiana* types, it collects debris on the leaf surface, whereas 'Thomas Hogg' does not.

Hosta leaves need not be broad to make their impact. An old favourite with cream margins is *H. sieboldii* (syn. *H. albomarginata*). *H. rohdeifolia* (syn. *H. helonioïdes*) *albopicta* has narrowly oblong blades with cream margins, the variegation extending down the flanged stalk. 'Ground Master' is a newer kind, excellent for massing, with its rather pale green, ivory-edged leaves. Two other variegated subspecies of *H. undulata*, known as *undulata* and *univittata*, have narrow, wavy, twisted leaves brightly splashed with creamy white.

Choice and colourful in the shade

Solomon's seal, with its arching stems and nodding ivory bells, is an elegant plant for shady places. There are two or three variegated Solomon's seals. One of the most striking is *Polygonatum* × *hybridum* 'Striatum' (also called 'Grace Barker' or

The star turn of this group is Hosta *'Gold Standard', its wide blades contrasting with a fern and the pink pokers of* Persicaria bistorta *'Superba'.*

'Variegatum'), the leaves of which are so streaked with cream as to leave little of the natural green. More discreet are *P. falcatum* 'Variegatum' and *P. odoratum* 'Variegatum', with a narrow white margin to the leaves. There are two variegated forms of lily-of-the-valley: *Convallaria majalis* 'Albostriata' with cream-striped leaves, and the scarce and lovely, yellow-streaked 'Vic Pawlowski's Gold'.

Well-behaved plants like these are good companions for the dark-leaved primrose, *Primula* 'Guinevere', its smoky-bronze leaves setting off lilac-pink flowers; and for the autumn-flowering *Saxifraga fortunei* 'Wada', which makes neat clumps of broad, mahogany-purple leaves. The white-splashed form of the mourning widow, *Geranium phaeum* 'Variegatum', would make a good taller companion, as much for its dark plum-purple flowers as for the foliage contrast. It is greatly superior to the cream-and-green *G. macrorrhizum* 'Variegatum'.

The brunneras, with their forget-me-not flowers in spring, have broad, bold leaves. There are two variegated forms: 'Hadspen Cream', margined with creamy yellow, and 'Dawson's White'. They burn easily in the wind or sun and like a reasonably moist soil. Even more magnificent than a well-grown brunnera is the big variegated comfrey, *Symphytum* × *uplandicum* 'Variegatum', the large leaves of which are broadly margined with cream. 'Goldsmith' is a lesser comfrey with cream variegations. The red-flowered lungwort, *Pulmonaria rubra*, has recently sported a white-margined form called 'David Ward'. Either this or the silvery pulmonarias could be grown alongside the dark-leaved wood spurge, *Euphorbia amygdaloïdes* 'Rubra', one of the few purples to keep its colour in shade.

LINKING SHADE PLANTINGS AND FLOWER BORDER

There is a whole class of shrubs with more or less commonplace leaves, redeemed by their colour or variegation, which can fittingly lead us from the idealized woodland of hostas and ferns to the border proper. Here coloured foliage can have an important role to play, dominating a scheme or acting as backdrop and context for the fleeting incidents of flower.

At the margins of the shadows cast by the tree canopy is the place to grow shrubs that need just the right balance between sun, for truly yellow leaf colour, and shade, to prevent scorching. The recipe for most deciduous shrubs with golden foliage is passing shade when the sun is at its highest; more shade is needed if you live in a hot, bright climate, less if your skies are perpetually rain-washed.

The golden mock orange, *Philadelphus coronarius* 'Aureus', has fresh, lime-yellow foliage and the bonus of sweet-scented, creamy flowers. Both *Weigela* 'Looymansii Aurea' and *Ribes sanguineum* 'Brocklebankii' disgrace themselves briefly when they bear pink flowers, which clash with their yellow foliage.

The golden dogwood, *Cornus alba* 'Aurea', is very appealing with its lime-yellow leaves and red winter stems; it is less declamatory than 'Spaethii', which is brightly green and yellow variegated. 'Elegantissima' is white margined. Other familiar shrubs have yellow forms: the hazel, *Corylus avellana* 'Aurea', and the guelder rose, *Viburnum opulus* 'Aureum'. Though evergreen, *Lonicera nitida* 'Baggesen's Gold' looks tatty in winter but, from spring to autumn, it is charming, with its spraying habit and neat leaves, clotted cream to yellow in the sun and lime green on the shady side. *Ligustrum* 'Vicaryi', with its yellow-suffused leaves, is even less surely evergreen, but handsome – like the more familiar golden privet, *L. ovalifolium* 'Aureum' – as a free-growing shrub rather than clipped.

The common elder, *Sambucus nigra*, has a number of fetching coloured forms, from the greeny-gold 'Aurea' and yellow-margined 'Aureomarginata' to ivory-edged 'Marginata' and 'Pulverulenta', in which the leaves are so heavily splashed with white that it looks as though someone has burst a flour-bag over it. Most striking of the elders grown for foliage are the cut-leaved *S. racemosa* 'Plumosa Aurea' and the newer, finer 'Sutherland Gold', bright as new-minted copper in spring and fading to plumes of gold. Cut them hard back each spring for the lushest and brightest foliage, and give them a well-nourished soil.

Much the same bronze and copper tints enliven *Physocarpus opulifolius* 'Luteus' and the newer 'Dart's Gold' in spring, before fading to bright yellow in summer. The yellow flowers of *Hypericum* × *inodorum* 'Summergold' blend with the chartreuse-yellow foliage, and the red fruits that follow in autumn are fun. At much the same level is the golden alpine currant, *Ribes alpinum* 'Aureum'.

The golden raspberry, *Rubus idaeus* 'Aureus', is altogether more inspiring and there is also a pretty golden bramble: *R. parviflorus* 'Sunshine Spreader', which makes a carpet of fresh lime-yellow in half shade or sun. There is now a golden form of the taller, whitewashed bramble, called *Rubus cockburnianus* 'Golden Vale'; the yellow leaves and white stems together are handsome, but it is very thorny and could be a menace in civilized settings. *R. thibetanus*, often descriptively labelled 'Silver Fern', also has white stems but so far only comes in grey; it is far better behaved. Little *Berberis thunbergii* 'Aurea' is also thorny and never outgrows its welcome; it needs shelter from icy winds and spring frosts as well as scorching sun but, with enough light to colour well, its rounded, lime-yellow leaves are as sunny as those of any golden shrub.

The yellow flowers of *Kerria japonica* 'Picta' are set off by jade green and white leaves on a green-stemmed bush. The variegated weigelas are pretty border shrubs, one creamy yellow on green (*Weigela florida* 'Variegata') and one white-margined (*W.* 'Praecox Variegata'); both have pale pink flowers. For foliage they are outshone by the variegated mock orange, *Philadelphus coronarius* 'Variegatus', also sometimes called 'Bowles's Variety'. It has the same creamy, powerfully fragrant flowers as the golden form but the foliage is broadly margined with pure white.

FOLIAGE IN THE FLOWER BORDERS

A shrub that has become very popular is *Abelia* × *grandiflora* 'Francis Mason', its glossy leaves, yellow-variegated with a rather metallic finish, contrasting with the pink and white flowers. It assorts well with fuchsias. And with the fuchsias we come to shrubs wholly appropriate to the flower border. If it is gold you want, you could choose *Fuchsia magellanica* 'Aurea' or 'Genii', both with lime-yellow foliage and typical red and violet fuchsia flowers – an oddly pleasing combination. There is a dainty, white-variegated fuchsia, *F. magellanica* (syn. *F. gracilis*) 'Variegata', very slender in red and purple flower, and another with cream edges which has sported from the pale-pink-flowered variety *molinae* and is known as 'Sharpitor'.

Fuchsia magellanica 'Versicolor' is one of two shrubs in the pink-grey-glaucous range that are perfect for linking shady and sunny sections of a border. In shade 'Versicolor' is grey with just a hint of pink; in the sun the pink tones intensify and dominate the grey. The other is *Rosa glauca* (syn. *R. rubrifolia*), grey-glaucous in the shade and flushed with purple on a blue-glaucous ground in the sun.

Full sun for the richest purple

Here, fully in the sun, is the place for purple foliage. No hardy shrub has produced so many purple forms as *Berberis thunbergii*, ranging from the little, bun-like 'Atropurpurea Nana' and 'Bagatelle', through the narrowly upright 'Helmond Pillar' and 'Red Pillar', to the spreading, very dark 'Dart's Red Lady' and older 'Red Chief' and, the original of them all, *B. thunbergii atropurpurea*. There are two basically purple, variegated cultivars: 'Rose Glow', all pink and cream on purple, and 'Harlequin' in pink, red and creamy yellow. 'Golden Ring', one of the larger cultivars, has maroon-red leaves with a fine gold margin. Bigger still, in dark purple, is the hybrid *B.* × *ottawensis* 'Superba', which has sported to 'Silver Mile' in which the purple is hazed and splashed with silver.

The purple hazel, *Corylus maxima* 'Purpurea', is a dark, looming presence with large, rounded leaves reaching their greatest size on coppiced plants. The purple elder, *Sambucus nigra* 'Guincho Purple' ('Purpurea') is a pleasant thing, of a rather metallic shade with little red in it. The flowers of *Weigela florida* 'Foliis Purpureis' are dusky deep pink and the foliage is a rather dim brown. For a much more insistent colour, choose the shrubby *Prunus* × *cistena*, in rich red-purple.

Best of all, though, are the Venetian sumachs, or smoke bushes. *Cotinus coggygria* comes in a number of purple forms, which if seed-raised can vary from milk chocolate to intense black-purple. Named selections are 'Royal Purple', 'Notcutt's Variety', the newer 'Velvet Cloak' and the hybrid 'Grace'. They all share the lovely quality of ruby translucence in spring when the young leaves unfurl. 'Royal Purple' is the perfect complement for one of the most striking barberries, *Berberis temolaica*, which has quite large, startlingly blue leaves.

Leaves of many colours

And so to a few multi-coloured and pink variegations. *Hypericum* × *moserianum* 'Tricolor' has been around for a long time, a low mound of a bush with leaves variegated white and pink on green. Another small shrub is the bramble *Rubus microphyllus* 'Variegatus', a dense clump of prickly stems set with bright little leaves, green splashed with pink and white to give an overall pink effect. There is a willow called *Salix integra* 'Hakuro-nishiki' ('Albomaculata' or 'Fuiri-koriyanagi'), which sells on sight in its bright pink and cream spring garb. *Spiraea* 'Pink Ice' also starts out pink and cream. The climbing *Actinidia kolomikta* has fairly large leaves, green at the stem end and pink and cream at the tip, sometimes covering as much as half the leaf, especially if it is grown on a sunny wall.

If you appreciate the winter tassels, rather like creamy catkins, of *Stachyurus chinensis* you might welcome its cream, pink and green variegated form 'Magpie'. Another winter-flowering shrub that has sported variegations is the cornelian cherry, *Cornus mas*. *C. mas* 'Variegata' has pure white variegations and shows up very well in shade, while 'Aureoelegantissima' has yellow margins to the leaves with a distinct pink flush.

Easy silvers and greys

Like purple foliage, the silvers and greys, with rare exceptions, are at their best in full sun. The silver shrub that everyone knows is *Brachyglottis* 'Sunshine' (syn. *Senecio laxifolius* or *S. greyi*). It is a lowish, mounded shrub with oval, leathery, grey-green leaves backed with white felt, and yellow daisies in summer if not hard pruned in spring.

Also silver, but entirely different in its lacy foliage, is *Artemisia* 'Powis Castle'. Furry, grey *Dorycnium hirsutum*, aromatic, grey *Caryopteris* × *clandonensis* with its haze of violet-blue flowers in late summer, silver, needle-leaved *Helichrysum italicum* with its curry aroma and stubby, platinum-leaved *H. splendidum*, all make spreading mounds for frontal positions. The cotton lavenders, or santolinas, have

The seductively undulating leaves of Elaeagnus commutata *glitter like polished silver in the sun.*

already crept into Chapter 2. Rue, *Ruta graveolens*, associates well with them; the best form is the very blue 'Jackman's Blue'.

Rather taller, and even more turpentiney aromatic than the caryopteris, is the Russian sage, *Perovskia atriplicifolia*, with toothed, grey leaves on white stems and spires of bright lavender-blue flowers. The shrubby potentillas are also invaluable for colder gardens. At least three are grey or silver in leaf: *Potentilla fruticosa* 'Manchu' in grey with white flowers, 'Beesii' in silver with bright yellow flowers, and 'Vilmoriniana' in silvery grey with white. 'Abbotswood Silver' is white-variegated.

Also deciduous and hardy are several small, grey or silver willows: *Salix lanata* with broad, grey-woolly leaves; *S. helvetica* with narrow, grey leaves; and *S. repens* var. *argentea* with smaller, grey-felted foliage and a more spraying, open habit of growth. Rather taller than these, the silver berry, *Elaeagnus commutata*, has bright, metallic-silver foliage and belongs to the select band of fully hardy, deciduous silvers. The tree purslane, *Atriplex halimus*, is an excellent coastal shrub with rhomboidal, silvery-grey leaves.

There are two larger willows of exceptional quality. The rosemary-leaved willow, *Salix elaeagnos*, makes a rounded bush with long, narrow needles, grey-green above and white below, which ruffle in the breeze. Even more silvery is *S. exigua*, a tall, narrow fountain of very slender leaves. It has the habit, curious in a willow, of suckering. So, too, does the sea buckthorn, *Hippophaë rhamnoïdes*, a tough and hardy shrub with narrow, grey leaves and, on female plants, soft-orange berries (provided that there is a male nearby to pollinate the flowers).

Also for the back of the border are the butterfly bushes. *Buddleja fallowiana* 'Alba' is at its best in mild areas, making a rather formless shrub redeemed by grey-white, felted foliage and scented, ivory-white flowers. 'Lochinch' is hardier but no less silvery pale; its flowers are ample spikes of clear violet-blue with the same honey perfume. These are both recognizably buddleias but, at first glance, *B. crispa* is very different, with its deeply toothed, white-woolly leaves on white-felted stems and short, cylindrical spikes of lilac flowers. With patience you can train *B. alternifolia* into a small, weeping tree with long trails of lavender flowers in late spring; it is worth choosing the form 'Argentea' for its silvery-silky foliage.

If the border is backed by a wall or runs along the base of a pergola, the silver and purple theme can be carried through with ornamental varieties of the grape vine, *Vitis vinifera*. 'Purpurea', the teinturier grape, has purple foliage, grey-bloomed when first unfurling, and the dusty miller vine, 'Incana', is pale with a grey-white bloom all season. Add fragrance with the silver jasmine, *Jasminum officinale* 'Argenteovariegatum' or, if your scheme includes yellow, with the vividly yellow-splashed *J. officinale* 'Aureum'.

THE ALL-ROUNDERS: BORDER PLANTS FOR LEAF AND FLOWER

Shrubs make a framework for the summer border within which flowers come and go. A surprising number of perennials have attractive leaves as well as flowers; they are doubly valuable, contributing both fleeting and longer-lasting colour.

The shrubs just described make the basis of a grey and silver border. Two colour ranges have emerged: lavender-blue and yellow. They are sympathetic to each other and you could build around the twin theme or isolate one or the other.

Silver with yellow

Achilleas, several of which have feathery, silver or grey foliage, belong with the yellow theme: *Achillea* 'Moonshine' in grey-green with flat, lemon flowerheads; 'Taygetea' in creamy primrose; and the fine, new 'Anthea' with silver foliage and pale yellow flowers. *Anthemis cupaniana* has stylish, white, yellow-eyed daisies in spring over wide mats of finely divided, silver-grey foliage. Later, the trefoil, silvery-silky leaves of *Potentilla atrosanguinea* var. *argyrophylla* form a plinth for yellow strawberry flowers; *P. atrosanguinea* itself has blood-red flowers.

The pearl everlastings, forms of *Anaphalis*, are useful both to quieten a bright scheme with their white, everlasting flowers and because they are unusual among greys in preferring a heavier, moister soil. *A. margaritacea* var. *cinnamomea* is the taller, with grey leaves, white-backed, on white stems; the palest grey form of *A. triplinervis* is 'Sommerschnee' ['Summer Snow']. *Helichrysum* 'Schweffellicht' ['Sulphur Light'] looks just like a lemon-yellow-flowered version of anaphalis. For some broad, simple leaves to contrast with the feathery achilleas and narrow anaphalises, there are two handsome hawkweeds: *Hieracium lanatum* with white-felted leaves; and *H. villosum*, which is more grey-woolly. Both have bright yellow flowers best removed unless you want seedlings.

Seed is also the way to raise the biennial mulleins, *Verbascum olympicum* and *V. bombyciferum*, valued for their rosettes of broad, white-felted leaves. Both have yellow flowers on tall spires. Another unusual plant with large leaves, blue-glaucous this time, is *Rudbeckia maxima*, a perennial with yellow, daisy flowers.

The giant meadow rue, *Thalictrum flavum* var. *glaucum*, has a similar colour scheme, with glaucous-blue leaves topped by a froth of lemon-green flowers.

Coming back down to earth, there are two very desirable spurges for the summer border with the usual lime-yellow flower bracts, set off by bright glaucous-blue foliage: *Euphorbia seguierana* ssp. *niciciana* with narrow, needle-like leaves and *E. nicaeënsis*, slightly taller with broader leaves. The spear leaves of *Sisyrinchium striatum* are blue-grey; though the plain-leaved form is not a patch on *S. striatum* 'Aunt May', in which the grey leaves are striped with cream. The trouble with *Aquilegia vulgaris* 'Woodside' is that not every plant sold under that name has the true indigo-blue flowers; but all should have leaves splashed and mottled creamy yellow on blue-green.

Self-contained colour schemes

The newly introduced *Centaurea montana* 'Gold Bullion' is a yellow-leaved form of another old favourite, the mountain knapweed; the combination of fresh chartreuse foliage and rich blue flowers is highly effective. Plants that create their own colour scheme with flower and leaf are always doubly welcome; so it is with *Crocosmia* × *crocosmiiflora* 'Solfaterre', a montbretia with flowers the colour of tangerine juice amid narrow, bronzed to milk-chocolate-brown sword leaves.

For a really bright scheme, there are two indispensables with purple foliage. *Lychnis* × *arkwrightii* has brilliant vermilion-scarlet flowers over dark leaves and *Oenothera fruticosa* 'Fyrverkeri' ['Fireworks'] has narrow, mahogany leaves to set off its bright yellow, evening-primrose flowers. If you have plenty of space, the reds and yellows can be cooled by the plume poppies. *Macleaya microcarpa* has pale coral plumes and *M. cordata* is white, with a pink-budded form, 'Flamingo'; the first has running roots, the second two make a compact clump. All have beautiful large, lobed leaves, grey-glaucous above and white beneath, on tall, white stems.

Silver, pink and lavender

If your taste runs more to lavender, mauve and pink than to yellow, you could choose instead, to add to your silvery theme, the dusty miller or the flower of Jove. The first is *Lychnis coronaria*, which has white-felted foliage as a plinth for brilliant magenta, pink, white or pink-centred white flowers. *L.* × *walkeri* 'Abbotswood Rose' is similar in rich pink. *L. flos-jovis* is shorter, with bright pink flowers and grey-woolly foliage. *Veronica spicata* var. *incana* allies spikes of bright blue, speedwell flowers to good, grey leaves, and the lamb's ears, *Stachys byzantina*, makes mats of white-woolly leaves with white-felted spikes of tiny mauve flowers. Many people prefer 'Silver Carpet', which does not flower. There is a little scabious, *S. graminifolia*, with very narrow, silver-grey leaves and lilac flowers all summer. One of the most enchanting of silver-leaved plants for small borders or raised beds is *Geranium traversii* var. *elegans*, which has rounded leaves and opaque, pale pink flowers.

Also in this colour range are border plants with glaucous foliage to add value in summer. *Erysimum* 'Bowles' Mauve', a perennial wallflower, performs so willingly all year with its narrow, steel-blue leaves and spires of rich lilac-purple

The golden garden at Crathes, in Scotland, is famous for its striking use of foliage in all the shades of yellow, bringing an echo of sunshine to the soft, blue-grey light of northern latitudes.

Exquisite though the fleur-de-lis flowers of bearded irises may be, when they are borne above the boldly cream-striped blades of Iris pallida *'Variegata', they take second place.*

flowers, that it may exhaust itself after a year or two. You need to take cuttings whenever you can to ensure a replacement. *E. linifolium* 'Variegatum' is ghostly pale by comparison, with grey leaves with wide ivory margins topped by lilac flowers.

Parahebe perfoliata is like a eucalyptus in blue-grey leaf, but the airy sprays of cool, blue-lilac flowers give the game away. Blue flowers, opening from pink buds, and glaucous leaves appear again in the spring-flowering *Mertensia ciliata*. There is a columbine, rather chubby with white or china-blue flowers but deriving its charm from glaucous-grey foliage; look for *Aquilegia flabellata* in any of its forms, including the ivory-white *pumila* var. *alba*. Miss Jekyll's tall, white columbine, *A. vulgaris* 'Nivea', also has distinctly grey foliage.

Then there is the noble *Iris pallida* var. *dalmatica*, a bearded iris with bold, long-lasting, blue-grey sword leaves and good, lilac-blue, fragrant flowers. Like the sisyrinchium already described (p.52), it has sported; not just one but two variegations, both of them superb: 'Variegata', striped with creamy yellow, and 'Argentea Variegata', striped with white. They all flower in early summer.

The flowers of the old ice plant, *Sedum spectabile*, do not make an appearance until late summer but, long before then, the fleshy, glaucous leaves have contributed to the border; so too, do those of the larger 'Herbstfreude' ['Autumn Joy']. 'Sunset Cloud' is smaller and its darkly glaucous leaves contrast with the pale jade of the ice plant. *S. alboroseum* 'Mediovariegatum' has fleshy, grey-green leaves with a conspicuous central splash of creamy yellow. The little 'Vera Jameson' is glaucous purple with garnet-pink flowers.

Leaves redeemed by variegations

It is time to mention a few more flowering plants that would hardly rate a second look for their leaves were it not for their variegations. One of the most outstanding is *Hemerocallis fulva* 'Kwanzo Variegata', in which the leaves are boldly ivory-striped. Also with sword leaves, though of different style in their glossy finish, is *Iris japonica*, delightful with its crested flowers but outstanding when these are combined, in 'Variegata', with white-striped foliage. *I. tectorum* 'Variegata' is smaller, with creamy variegations. The much narrower, strap-shaped leaves of *Tulbaghia violacea* are quite pretty in their natural, rather grey-glaucous colouring that blends well with the lilac, agapanthus-like flowers, but 'Silver Lace', with white-striped foliage, is enchanting.

There are two stunning white-variegated phloxes: 'Norah Leigh' with pale lilac flowers and 'Harlequin' with bright purple flowers. The obedient plant, *Physostegia virginiana* 'Variegata', is also very white in leaf, with rose-pink flowers. Fit for the same range of colours is *Veronica gentianoïdes* 'Variegata', its pale blue spires borne over glossy, cream-splashed leaves.

Mainly about leaves

Call cow parsley 'Queen Anne's lace' and it at once sounds more appealing, but call it *Anthriscus sylvestris* 'Ravenswing' and you have a picture of glossy, feathery foliage, bronzed deepening to purple-black, forming a plinth for the lacy flowers. A selected form of wormwood, *Artemisia absinthium*, leans towards another metal, not bronze but pewter grey; it is called 'Lambrook Silver'. All the forms of *A. ludoviciana* are more truly silver; the leaves vary from narrow and willowy to jagged-edged in *latiloba* and finely cut in 'Silver Queen'.

A 'weed' that has given us a purple-leaved version is the plantain; *Plantago major* 'Rubrifolia' has wide, ribbed leaves of reddish maroon, and seeds more or less true. There is, incidentally, more than one variegated plantain, including *P. asiatica* 'Variegata', which is grey-green striped with white. Feverfew in its green form is undistinguished but the golden-leaved *Chrysanthemum* (syn. *Tanacetum*) *parthenium* 'Aureum' is bright and cheerful, and it also seeds true.

The leaves of *Euphorbia dulcis* 'Chameleon' transform an unexciting, green-flowered spurge into a first-rate foliage plant, for they are deep, velvety, chocolate-purple. The best forms of *Heuchera micrantha* 'Palace Purple' are also very dark, with a glossy finish to the broad, lobed leaves; seedlings vary from bronze and milk chocolate to the true deep purple and are stunning with blue-glaucous or silver foliage, a blue grass perhaps or a lacy artemisia. Another textural contrast comes from the foliage of the bronze fennel, *Foeniculum vulgare* 'Purpureum', which is as brown as a fox's brush when first unfolding, expanding to purple threads beneath the yellow, cow parsley flowers. Different again is the fleshy, succulent texture of the sedums. *Sedum telephium* ssp. *maximum* 'Atropurpureum' has dark, bloomy, purple leaves.

Fig 10 *Everyone loves a lucky four-leaved clover; when it comes blotched with rich, dark-chocolate tones, as in* Trifolium repens *'Purpurascens Quadrifolium', it brings good looks as well as good fortune to the garden.*

In *Houttuynia cordata* 'Chameleon', the single flowers are nothing against the leaves, where yellow, red, copper and pink jostle with green for space. At its most lush and quietest in cool shade, it is painfully bright grown in full sun. The larger *Persicaria* (syn. *Tovara*) *virginiana* 'Painter's Palette' has bold leaves striped with creamy yellow and marked, midway along the blade, with a mahogany-red chevron. Without the chevron, it is called simply 'Variegata'.

Embroidering the ground

At the front of your borders, or running back among taller plants, you may wish to weave tapestries of colour, as fine as needlepoint embroidery.

Right at the beginning of the alphabet come the acaenas, small, carpeting New Zealanders with tiny, divided leaves, steely blue-grey in *Acaena* 'Blue Haze', verdigris blue in *A. buchananii*. They contrast strikingly with the larger leaves of the purple ajugas, such as *Ajuga reptans* 'Atropurpurea', which have an almost metallic finish. Give them sun for the best colouring. There are multi-coloured ajugas too: 'Burgundy Glow', with leaves almost wholly magenta, rose and cream; and 'Multicolor' or 'Rainbow' (which you may also find labelled 'Tricolor'; all three names are used, but there is only one plant), a curious mixture of bronze, pink, yellow and cream. 'Delight' has grey, pink and cream leaves, very pretty if you want to spread a pale carpet – around the tiny, purple *Phormium* 'Thumbelina', perhaps, or among bergenias. Palest of all is 'Variegata', in grey-green and ivory.

Few gardeners would welcome the green-leaved ground elder into their gardens but the variegated form, *Aegopodium podagraria* 'Variegata', is very fresh with its cream and jade leaves, and not so much of a spreader. The variegated ground ivy, *Glechoma hederacea* 'Variegata', is another wildling tamed, with rounded leaves margined white on trailing stems. The purple clover also spreads willingly: *Trifolium repens* 'Purpurascens' has the standard three leaflets and 'Purpurascens Quadrifolium' is four-leaved; both forms are chocolate-purple with a green margin.

Grasses in the border

Amid succulent, lacy or glossy leaves, grasses provide the contrast of their narrow blades, which, whether erect or arching, contribute an essentially vertical line to the border. Many of the smaller grasses and sedges can be used to make edgings, colour bands or patches of colour drifting back among taller plants; the larger grasses are ideal to soar above low plantings of rounded outlines.

There are no truly silver grasses but several are intensely blue, none more so than the little, thread-fine fescues, which are delightful massed with purple foliage. *Festuca amethystina*, as its name suggests, has a definite touch of lilac in its glaucous foliage, while *F. glauca* is bluer; bluest of all is 'Blaufuchs' ['Blue Fox']. There is a very blue-silver form of *F. valesiaca* too, called 'Silbersee' ['Silver Sea'].

White-variegated grasses develop their best colour – or lack of it – in full light, but are valuable for bringing a pale note to lightly shaded places. One of the whitest is *Arrhenantherum elatius* ssp. *bulbosum* 'Variegatum', which has long, narrow blades about 30 cm (12 in) long and is easily increased by the bulbils that form at the base of the stems; it is not invasive. Almost as white is *Holcus mollis* 'Variegatus', which runs, but very slowly. *Dactylis glomerata* 'Variegata' is a white-variegated clump-former. The variegated purple moor grass, *Molinia caerulea* 'Variegata', actually prefers light shade, where it make dense tufts of cream-striped, arching blades that fade to parchment in autumn and last well into winter.

Soft harmonies of blue-grey are fresh and cool beneath the summer sun. Helictotrichon sempervirens *makes a wind-ruffled carpet of fine blades beneath the neat pyramid of* Cupressus arizonica var. glabra.

Grasses with all-yellow or yellow-variegated leaves, with the odd exception, need the sun to develop their brightest colouring. The golden foxtail grass, *Alopecurus pratensis* 'Aureus', is an intense, brilliant yellow. It makes 30 cm (12 in) tufts that spread only slowly. The green- and gold-striped foxtail is *A. pratensis* 'Aureovariegatus'. There is a form of the wavy hair grass, *Deschampsia flexuosa* 'Tatra Gold', which is at its most yellow in spring, turning to lime yellow in summer. *Hakonechloa macra* 'Aureola' and *H. macra* 'Alboaurea' are almost as bright as the foxtails, with their vivid yellow stripes on arching blades that compose a graceful mound. The blades become stained with maroon as summer advances. Both prefer light shade and look superb with hostas – blue for contrast of line and colour; yellow or yellow and green to point up the difference of outline.

'Sedge' is an even more banal-sounding word than 'grass' but among the sedges are some outstanding garden plants. *Carex buchananii* has hair-like leaves of bronze and pale coppery pink, making an erect 60 cm (2 ft) clump, while the bronze form of *C. comans* has weeping, hair-fine blades of grey-bronze to blonde. *C. flagellifera* is midway in size, a mound of narrow, pale bronze blades.

Among the bigger grasses are some clump-formers, ideal as specimens in the border, and a few runners with territorial ambitions. The blue-glaucous lyme grass, *Leymus* (syn. *Elymus*) *arenarius*, spreads like a giant couch or twitch, and the yellow-striped *Spartina pectinata* 'Aureomarginata' is almost as bad. The old gardener's garters, *Phalaris arundinacea* 'Picta', with white-striped blades, is another energetic runner but the newer version, 'Feesey' is more stay-at-home, probably because it has more white on the blades and thus less vigour.

All the variants of miscanthus are clump-formers with no land-grabbing tendencies and all are handsome specimens forming graceful fountains of foliage. *Miscanthus sinensis* 'Variegatus' has white-striped blades, while 'Zebrinus', unusually, is horizontally banded in yellow. *M. sinensis* var. *purpurascens* is shorter than these and subtly coloured, brown with a pink midrib. A bigger clump is made by the pampas grass, *Cortaderia selloana* 'Gold Band'; here the name describes vertical, not horizontal, stripes. Like all pampas grasses, it is viciously sharp and must be handled only with thick gloves. For sheer magnificence there is *Arundo donax* 'Variegata', which is unfortunately rather frost-tender, but worth cosseting for its soaring, blue-grey blades boldly striped with ivory.

If you want a medium-sized, blue-glaucous grass that does not take over the garden, there are several to choose from. *Helictotrichon sempervirens* has needle-like, erect leaves topped by grey flowers. Though related to the lyme grass, *Elymus hispidus* (syn. *Agropyron glaucus*) is well-behaved and very blue, as is *E. magellanicus* (syn. *A. pubiflorum*). The naming is slightly confused, and there may be three plants, perhaps even more, under these names. Beware of the name *Elymus glaucus*, which is sometimes used for the invasive lyme grass.

Most bamboos are outside the scope of this book but there are two of restrained growth that are variegated. You may find them listed under *Arundinaria*, but current thinking is that they are *Pleioblastus auricomus* (syn. *A. viridistriatus*) and *P. variegatus* (syn. *A. fortunei*). The first has yellow stripes with sometimes half the leaf, from base to tip, entirely golden; the second is white-striated.

CHAPTER 5

SUMMER LEAVES FOR SPECIAL SITUATIONS

THE TREES ARE in full sail and the borders bursting with leaves of many colours but there are more summer leaves to consider. You may have space for no more than one or two of the bigger foliage plants and want to make miniature plantings in the same colourful idiom. Perhaps you have a rock garden that you want to make colourful and easy to care for; the little plants can be your allies in this too. Or perhaps you have a hot, dry corner where plants like hostas shrivel and die, or a soggy patch which seems to grow more weeds than anything else. Here too, foliage plants can come to your rescue.

FOR SMALLER SPACES

Among what are loosely known as 'rock plants' are several with colourful foliage that would be swamped in all but the smallest border. They can well be grown in a rock garden or a raised bed, or even in a trough. Among these are some silver-leaved plants, diminutive cousins of the silvers and greys we grow in our borders. *Euryops acraeus* is one of the most silvery shrubs we can grow outside frost-free areas, forming a small mound of platinum-pale, needle leaves. The silver of *Artemisia schmidtiana* 'Nana' is touched with grey; it is the texture, above all, of this small spreader that appeals for its finely divided leaves are as soft as silk. Two similar small plants, often still listed under *Chrysanthemum* but now called *Tanacetum densum* ssp. *amani* and *T. herderi*, make mats of silver-grey foliage resembling Prince-of-Wales feathers. Several small achilleas – *Achillea argentea* (syn. *A. clavennae*) in silver, *A.* x *lewisii* 'King Edward' in grey, and others – make smaller, neater mats. *Antennaria dioica* is markedly grey in leaf too. One of the smallest of silvers is *Raoulia hookeri* (syn. *R. australis*), a hard film of tiny leaves spangled, at flowering time, with minute, yellow flowers. The small *Aethionema* 'Warley Rose' combines blue-grey leaves with bright rose-pink flowers.

All these like sun and well-drained soil, with or without lime, but *Cyathodes colensoi* must have a lime-free soil. It is a small, spreading shrub with leaves of a curious grey-mauve-glaucous tint. Cool but free-draining soil suits *Celmisia coriacea*, which makes in miniature something of the effect of an astelia, with its rosettes of silvery, pointed, broadsword leaves.

As well as the larger border sedums, or stonecrops, there are many smaller ones ideal for tumbling about among rocks. *Sedum anacampseros* has small, blue-grey leaves, while *S. spathulifolium* makes flat rosettes of blunt leaves, richly purple in 'Purpureum' and bloomed with white meal in 'Cape Blanco'. The rounded, blue-glaucous leaves of *S. cauticola* are borne on trailing stems; the plant is a little like *S. sieboldii*, which, in its cream-splashed form, is often grown as a house plant. Another trailer is *S. spurium*, which has a dark-leaved form, 'Purpurteppich' ['Purple Carpet']. In complete contrast, *S. acre* 'Aureum' has tiny, yellow-tipped leaves. The plain green form is known as 'wall pepper' and is busily invasive, as every little brittle leaf that breaks off makes a new plant, but the golden form is well behaved.

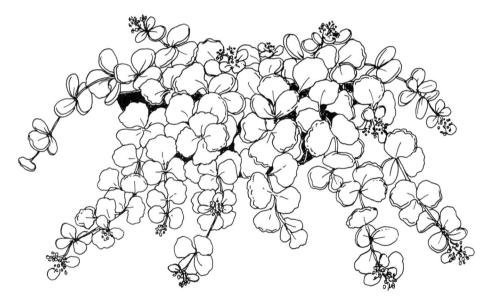

Fig 11 *Often grown as a house or conservatory plant, especially in its cream-blotched form 'Mediovariegatum',* Sedum sieboldii *lends itself well to hanging baskets, where its arching stems and blue-grey, succulent leaves show to best advantage.*

You would need to keep snow-in-summer, *Cerastium tomentosum* var. *columnae*, well away from these small things, even the easy-growing *Sedum spurium*, for it is a rampageous spreader, though attractive with its silver-grey leaves and white flowers. A dry-stone wall whence it cannot spread into choicer things is a good place for it. Old walls, too, make a good home for yellow alyssum, *Alyssum saxatile* (syn. *Aurinia saxatilis*), which has narrow, grey leaves.

There is a variegated alyssum, 'Dudley Neville Variegated', which is very fetching with cream and grey foliage and amber flowers, as well as variegations in those other two ever-popular rock plants, aubrieta and arabis. *Aubrieta* 'Aureovariegata' has yellow-margined leaves and lilac flowers, 'Argenteovariegata' is white-edged. The little, carpeting *Arabis ferdinandi-coburgii* comes in two styles:

'Old Gold', with leaves edged yellow, and 'Variegata' with white-edged leaves. *A. caucasica* 'Variegata' is a bigger plant with cream-splashed foliage.

Later, in summer, the blue stars of *Campanula garganica* open. 'Dickson's Gold' has the further appeal of bright yellow foliage. Yellow, too, is the colour of the mossy saxifrage 'Cloth of Gold', but it is rather a tricky customer and I have never seen it spread cloths any bigger than a small handkerchief.

The trouble with *Geranium sessiliflorum* 'Nigrescens' is its big tap root and its tendency to seed into the heart of other plants. But it is very charming, with its flat rosettes of crinkle-edged, chocolate-brown leaves. Foliage of dark colouring is not common among little plants but among the select few is a celandine, *Ranunculus ficaria* 'Brazen Hussy', not invasive like the green-leaved weed but very desirable with its sheeny-yellow stars against almost black leaves.

THE COLOURED HERB GARDEN

The thymes, plain or coloured, are often grown among rock plants, and there is nothing wrong with that. But as herbs, they are joined by other aromatic plants

Herbs are not just for flavour on the table; they can make garden pictures too, as in this potager-style herb garden, where golden lemon balm is the vivid centrepiece.

less attractive unless in their coloured-foliage forms. Nobody would grow plain green lemon balm or marjoram except for their flavour but you can have both flavour and colour. Many variants are pretty enough to grow in the flower border.

There are at least two all-gold thymes – *Thymus × citriodorus* 'Aureus' and 'Bertram Anderson' – and another two with yellow variegations – *T. × citriodorus* 'Golden King' and 'Doone Valley'. For a paler effect there are white-variegated thymes, *T. × citriodorus* 'Silver Queen' and *T. vulgaris* 'Silver Posie', in which the tiny, lilac-pink flowers make a charming picture. The golden marjoram, *Origanum vulgare* 'Aureum', is one of those maddening plants that scorches in hot sun but turns green in the shade.

The golden balms, *Melissa officinalis* 'Aurea' and the more wholehearted 'All Gold', definitely need some shade to avoid scorch. They have the same curiously synthetic lemon fragrance as the green type, and the same free-seeding habits, only worse, because all the seedlings will be green. Deadhead them rigorously if you decide they are worth it. The variegated apple mint, *Mentha suaveolens* (syn. *M. rotundifolia*) 'Variegata', is so much splashed with cream that some shoots are entirely albino; it makes an insipid sauce but is too pretty to omit.

Back in the sun, you do not need to grow the ordinary culinary sage if you like sage and onion stuffing because the coloured forms do just as well. *Salvia officinalis* 'Purpurascens' is evergreen, though tatty in winter; it brings an unusual note of greyish purple to the garden, just the thing with pink roses and silver foliage. 'Tricolor' is smaller in growth and a bit frost-tender; the leaves are grey, purple and cream. In the other half of the spectrum, 'Icterina' is a green and gold sage.

As a centrepiece for this many-coloured herb garden, you could grow a golden bay, *Laurus nobilis* 'Aurea', which is more of a yellow-green than really yellow but is a good evergreen that, with great patience, you could turn into a pyramid or dome just as is sometimes done with the green bay. And there, with curled parsley for looks or flat-leaved parsley for flavour, and perhaps a few plants of the black-leaved basil, *Ocimum basilicum* 'Dark Opal', are most of the herbs you need for salads or *bouquet garni*.

HOT AND DRY

Being native to the Mediterranean region, culinary sage is well adapted to spells of drought and dislikes wet, cold soil. The narrow-leaved, grey-green *Salvia lavandulifolia* is also one for full sun in drained soil. These and many other Mediterraneans are evergreen but, in cooler, damper climates, they seldom look their best in winter. In complete contrast to these woody plants, *Salvia argentea* is an herbaceous sage, forming rosettes of broad, white-cobwebbed leaves.

The lavenders are southerners too. Of the common lavenders, those selected for their flowers mostly have indifferent foliage; the greyest is the old *Lavandula × intermedia* Dutch group, with rather broad leaves. It is quite outshone by the more tender *L. lanata*, with narrow, white-woolly leaves, and *L. dentata* var. *candicans*, which is just as white but with toothed leaves. Both like it hot and dry.

The Jerusalem sage, *Phlomis fruticosa*, is greyish green, but much whiter is the pink-flowered *P. italica*, with pointed, woolly leaves. In the same colour range,

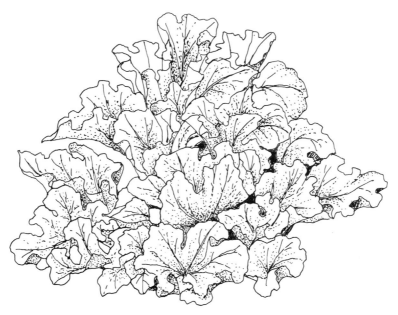

Fig 12 *A delicious vegetable when blanched, sea kale* (Crambe maritima) *is also a remarkable foliage plant, with large, deeply lobed and crinkled, glaucous-white leaves.*

Cistus albidus has white-woolly foliage and mauve-pink, crumpled-silk flowers. Even more appealing is the satiny-silver foliage of *Convolvulus cneorum*, a small shrub with fluted, white trumpets opening from pink buds. From North Africa comes *Teucrium fruticans*, a delightful small shrub of open habit with grey leaves on white stems and lavender-blue flowers.

A silvery plant that will sprawl through its neighbours is *Senecio viravira* (syn. *S. leucostachys*), with comb-like leaves and pleasant, creamy flower heads rather than the more usual yellow daisies. Another sprawler is *Artemisia arborescens*, whose leaves are even more finely divided than the senecio and palely silvery silky. *Ballota pseudodictamnus* has rounded, woolly leaves on pipe-cleaner stems, while *B. acetabulosa* is no less grey but more crinkled in leaf.

The rock roses, *Helianthemum*, come in a range of sizes and flower colours; they are ideal for tumbling over rocks or dry banks in full sun and some have grey foliage. They are cheerful but undistinguished and you might prefer the more aristocratic *Halimium ocymoïdes*, a grey-white mound with clear yellow, black-eyed flowers. A size up from this, *H. lasianthum* is also grey, with yellow flowers, either stainless or black-blotched. *H. halimifolium* has narrow leaves and, finest (and tenderest) of all, *H. atriplicifolium* has broadly rhomboidal, intensely silvered leaves. To contrast in outline, but not colour, with all these, *Artemisia splendens* has leaves like twisted silver wire and *A. stelleriana* is a sprawler with lobed, grey-white leaves. 'Mori' is a neater, whiter version.

Cytisus battandieri is a North African broom, but surprisingly hardy, and handsome with its leaves of three silver-grey leaflets and tubby spikes of yellow, pineapple-scented flowers. It is often grown on a wall but is far more impressive free-standing.

The coronillas are pretty shrubs related to the brooms, with yellow, fragrant pea flowers. Both *Coronilla valentina* and the larger *C. valentina* ssp. *glauca* have divided leaves of distinctly glaucous tint. 'Variegata' is even daintier, the leaves variegated with cream on blue-grey, and so airy it might be about to take flight.

Plants of the seashore, even of cool, temperate regions, also do well in the hotter, drier places. The sea holly, *Eryngium maritimum*, is glaucous white in leaf and bract, and sea kale (*Crambe maritima*) has great, lobed, grey-white leaves. The horned poppies, *Glaucium flavum* in yellow and the burnt-orange *G. corniculatum*, are biennials forming rosettes of deeply crinkled, bright blue-grey leaves. Around all these, *Omphalodes linifolia*, an annual with grey-glaucous leaves and milk-white flowers, should seed itself.

DAMP AND JUNGLY

In contrast to these children of the sun are the lush, leafy plants that revel in damp soil. With one exception, you should forget the greys and silvers, but there is plenty else to tempt. The exception is *Lysimachia ephemerum*, a tall, slender perennial with glaucous foliage and white flowers in spires, the overall effect being distinctly grey. It cools the strong colours of lobelias while echoing their upright lines. These are not, of course, the blue lobelias of hanging baskets but the perennials, such as 'Queen Victoria' and 'Bees' Flame' with brilliant scarlet flowers, or 'Dark Crusader' with ruby-crimson flowers; all three are endowed with deep beetroot-purple foliage.

The reverse of the big, rounded leaves of *Ligularia dentata* 'Othello' and 'Desdemona' is glossy, maroon-purple and the flowers are bold, orange-yellow daisies. For a strong combination, plant them in association with Mr Bowles's golden sedge, *Carex elata* (syn. *C. stricta*) 'Aurea', the narrow blades of which are more yellow than green. They also look magnificent with the figwort, *Scrophularia auriculata* 'Variegata', with its crinkly leaves boldly splashed with cream.

Less markedly coloured, but striking in outline, are the big, digitate, web-footed leaves of *Rodgersia podophylla*, bronzed in spring and autumn, and even in summer if grown in full sun in the damp soil it appreciates. It associates well with one of the sedges, the broad-bladed, cream-margined *Carex siderosticha* 'Variegata'. Full light and damp soil give the best results with two more properly purple-leaved perennials, *Artemisia kitadakensis* 'Guizhou' and *Cimicifuga simplex* Atropurpurea group. The first has deeply cut, fern-like, almost black leaves with an undertone of green; the second, one of the bugbanes, also has dissected leaves, of chocolate-purple colouring, topped by tall spires of white flowers opening from dark buds. *C. simplex* 'Brunette' is extra dark in leaf.

Carex riparia 'Variegata', in which the narrow blades are white with a fine green margin, looks well with these dark leaves but, be warned: it is invasive. A safer choice would be the sweet flag, *Acorus calamus* 'Variegatus', which has iris-like leaves striped with cream and enjoys damp soil or even a bog. There are two true irises for damp places which have variants that do not turn green in summer: the Japanese water iris, *I. ensata* (syn. *I. kaempferi*) 'Variegata', and the more striking *I. laevigata* 'Variegata' with creamy-white stripes along the leaves.

The bold, web-footed leaves of Rodgersia podophylla *are at their best in moist soil in sun, where they take on rich, bronzed tones.*

TENDERS AND EPHEMERALS IN THE SUMMER GARDEN

With all these riches, why grow tender plants or bother with annuals? Not everyone does, of course. But if you enjoy experimenting with colours and textures and outlines, or like to vary your container plantings from year to year, sooner or later you are likely to be tempted by a plant that falls into these groups.

A plant that may have architecture thrust upon it is *Helichrysum petiolare*. However often one sees it, this remains an essential component for anyone planning their containers for summer; it is also invaluable in the border, with its spraying, interweaving habit and rounded, grey-felted leaves. If you train the main stem upwards on a cane, it will grow to 90 cm (3 ft) or so in a season, with the side branches standing out almost horizontally; in this shape it makes a delightful centrepiece for a frothy planting of, for example, pink, ivy-leaved geraniums, or bedding verbenas. It has an appealing variegated form, all cream and grey, while 'Limelight' is a uniform, soft butter to chartreuse yellow, best in passing shade and disliking to be dry at the root. *Plecostachys serpyllifolia*, often listed as *Helichrysum microphyllum*, is in effect a dwarf, tiny-leaved version of the grey form.

With frost-free shelter for the winter, and patience, you can turn the Paris daisies into standards but they are just as pretty when bushy, especially if you choose *Argyranthemum foeniculaceum* 'Royal Haze' for its thread-fine, blue-grey leaves. The delightful *A. maderense* is naturally dwarf and combines dissected, blue-grey foliage with primrose daisies.

In complete contrast to these feathery leaves are the huge, paddle-shaped, smooth-textured blades of cannas. As well as the usual green, there are some with rich purple foliage. *Canna indica* 'Purpurea' has leaves slightly narrower than those of hybrids such as 'Wyoming' and 'Roi Humbert'. Another, *C. malawiensis* 'Variegata', has the same big paddles with yellow stripes angling off from the midrib. One of the ginger lilies, *Hedychium greenei*, is in a similar idiom to the cannas, with narrower, but still bold, pointed blades, held very erect to reveal the glossy, mahogany reverse.

A variegated osteospermum would be another possible companion for the purple cannas. *Osteospermum* 'Bodegas Pink' has leaves variegated creamy yellow, but pink flowers are not the happiest choice to go with red- or yellow-flowered cannas, so I would choose 'Silver Sparkler', which has a nice, tumbling habit, white-variegated leaves and white, blue-backed flowers. Smaller and neater than these, *Felicia amelloïdes* 'Variegata' has blunt, cream-variegated leaves and daisies of the most innocent sky blue imaginable. Another plant that makes a fine companion for the cannas, contrasting in colour, outline and texture, is *Lotus berthelotii*, which has softly silky, intensely silvered, needle leaves on flowing stems and coppery-scarlet, claw flowers.

In the same colour range as the purple cannas is that apparently indestructible dahlia, 'Bishop of Llandaff'. Its flowers are rich, bright scarlet, set off by deeply cut, glossy, almost metallic black-purple leaves. The smooth leaves of *Iresine herbstii* are red-purple and those of *I. lindenii* rather deeper beetroot; they also differ slightly in leaf shape, the first with blunt tips and the second pointed. *I. herbstii* 'Brilliantissima' is deep purple with red veins and 'Aureoreticulata' is even more striking in yellow with red veins. The frilly-leaved *Perilla frutescens* var. *nankinensis* is bronze-purple and about twice as tall as the iresines at 90 cm (3 ft). It has to be grown from seed and is tricky to raise but worth it.

Coleus are also often raised from seed and their colours – not to mention the different leaf forms, plain or crinkled – can be very brilliant, in reds and yellows, oranges and near-blacks. The best can be increased by cuttings and there are named kinds as well, including self-chartreuse yellows, all-black, velvety crimson, and sundry variegations. Variegated pelargoniums must be grown from cuttings. *Pelargonium* × *hortorum* 'Mrs Henry Cox' is as multi-coloured as they come, with white, cream, yellow, pink, red and purple as well as green, and is best as a single plant to be admired at close quarters, 'Maréchal MacMahon' ('The Czar') is effective in a mass, with its concentric bands of yellow, terracotta and maroon filling the rounded leaf.

A plant which I like to grow in a container to stand in a sheltered corner of a patio is *Ampelopsis brevipedunculata* 'Elegans'. This is a climber but of weak growth

Opposite: *The huge leaves of the banana,* Ensete ventricosum, *set off the vivid flowers and big paddle leaves of cannas in a London garden.*

Rex begonias, so familiar as house plants, add an exotic note in the garden as their metallic-silver, pewter and crimson, boldly marked leaves spill out of a stone trough.

well suited to flopping over the sides of a big pot, where its small leaves, so heavily splashed with pink and cream that there is virtually no green left, can be enjoyed close at hand.

One of the most stunning variegated plants for frost-free gardening is *Metrosideros kermadecensis* 'Variegatus', whose scarlet, bottlebrush flowers are set amid yellow-margined leaves. ('Radiant' has the opposite variegation: yellow with a green edge.) It needs a quiet or sombre setting: the plain purple iresines would be about as emphatic as you would want to go.

Foliage plants for in-and-out gardening

As well as making big, bold sweeps or careful patterns in traditional or modernist bedding style, you can use your tenders and ephemerals to add substance and colour to the summer border (and to plug unwanted gaps). In a silver and yellow scheme, you could add *Gazania* 'Silver Beauty' for its deeply lobed leaves and bright yellow flowers, or the quieter 'Cream Beauty'. Gazanias are surprisingly tolerant of heavy, though not wet, soils, but must have full sun. The silvery, filigree *Senecio cineraria* is usually offered in its very white but slightly less finely divided form 'White Diamond', which survives mild winters; it should be cut hard back, after the risk of frost, unless you decide to throw it out.

In mild areas the more tender hebes, derived from *Hebe speciosa* and grown for their showy spikes of fragrant flowers, will survive the winter. Elsewhere they can

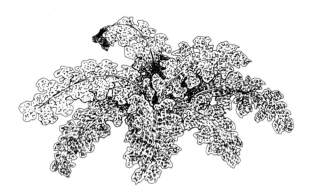

Fig 13 *The common names of this attractive thistle,* Silybum marianum, *reflect the legend that its white blotches are drops of the Virgin Mary's milk: milk thistle, Our Lady's Thistle and blessed thistle are just some of these.*

be grown afresh each year from cuttings. This is the way to treat *H. speciosa* 'Tricolor', which has grey-green, cream and pink to blackcurrant-purple leaves (and purple flower spikes), and the wholly lovely *H. × andersonii* 'Variegata', which has pretty, fragrant spikes of lavender blue and leaves bordered with ivory white that spreads over the central green to give a range of subtle shades of jade and grey.

Eucalyptus globulus used to be much used as a dot plant in bedding schemes, on account of its intensely blue-silver juvenile foliage. It is easy from seed; in mild areas it makes a large tree extremely quickly. There is no reason why you should not grow the blue, feathery *Acacia baileyana* from seed and bed it out, too. The variegated abutilons are also used as dot plants and they also work well as the centrepiece of a sizeable container-planting. *Abutilon megapoticum* 'Variegatum' has leaves mottled with yellow and narrow-waisted, red and yellow flowers; *A. × milleri* 'Variegatum' is similar in leaf and slightly larger in flower.

Self-sowing annuals and biennials

Some plants are obliging enough to sow themselves, so once having introduced them into the garden, you can leave them alone thereafter, except to remove surplus seedlings. The purple *Atriplex hortensis* var. *rubra* looks after itself in this way, decorating every corner in which it lands with blood-red leaves. It is related to the ruby, or rhubarb, chard, a highly ornamental vegetable with dark leaves enlivened by a broad, scarlet midrib. The Scotch thistle, *Onopordum acanthium*, is so dominant in flower, reaching 2.1 m (7 ft) or more, that one or two are enough; but it is hardly possible to have too many of the magnificent silvery rosettes it makes in its first season. At a much more modest level, the milk thistle, *Silybum marianum*, has leaves marbled and splashed with white.

It is unusual for variegated plants to come true from seed but among those which do are two pretty annuals. *Tropaeolum majus* 'Alaska' is a nasturtium with the usual orange, spurred flowers and rounded leaves, which are speckled with cream. The leaves of *Euphorbia marginata* are white-variegated, with hardly any green remaining.

CHAPTER 6

AUTUMN TINTS

FOR SOME PEOPLE, autumn is a melancholy season, as the nights draw in and the dread of winter cold begins to fill their minds. Yet it is one of the most colourful seasons in the garden. Well, say the pessimists, that is true, but it is all over so quickly, the leaves fall almost as soon as they have turned colour. Keen gardeners know they can confound that argument too; not every tree, shrub or perennial that flares up in autumn does so at the precise same moment. If you choose carefully, you can have weeks of autumn brilliance.

In cool, temperate climates where the seasons are sharply defined, such as those of north-eastern North America, autumn colour is reliable. In the UK, with its blurred transitions from spring to summer and summer to autumn, the display can be outstanding one year and disappointing the next. Nonetheless, some trees and shrubs can be relied on to perform in all but the most inimical seasons.

DOUBLE-VALUE TREES AND SHRUBS

Unless you have wide acres to fill, trees and shrubs – especially the larger ones – that do nothing much except colour up in autumn are not worth their space. But a tree that looks good all year, even if it is 'only' green in summer and flares up brightly in autumn, is another matter. So it is with many of the maples. Among those of small-tree size, the snake-barks offer vivid autumn tints, attractive bark and leaves making beautiful patterns of light and shadow. Most of them turn to shades of crimson and scarlet. The choice lies between: *Acer capillipes*; *A. davidii* and its selected forms 'Ernest Wilson', 'George Forrest' and 'Serpentine'; *A. grosseri* var. *hersii*; and *A. rufinerve*, which adds yellow to its pyrotechnics. *A. pensylvanicum* is more apt to turn entirely yellow. The paperbark maple, *A. griseum*, is renowned for its shaggy, mahogany-brown trunk and branches; its neatly three-lobed leaves are second to none in their crimson, scarlet and orange fall tones. It has a less familiar relative in the Nikko maple, *A. maximowiczianum* (syn. *A. nikoense*), which lacks the lovely bark but is no less bright in leaf.

All these make trees of modest size, casting friendly shade for more lowly foliage plants. I shall recommend just one larger maple for autumn colour: the red maple, *Acer rubrum*, and in particular its selected form 'October Glory', which colours to a deep, rich crimson-scarlet, the change from green starting later than most and lasting long.

We have already met the Japanese maples, *Acer palmatum*, and the full-moon maple, *A. japonicum*, in a variety of guises, so it should come as no surprise to find them here as well. After their summer stint as foliage plants par excellence, they prove that they can surpass any tree or shrub in their autumn brilliance. Any Japanese maple you choose will turn incandescent in autumn but one above all is renowned for its brilliance: 'Osakazuki', a pure and glowing scarlet. Unusually, the coral-stemmed 'Senkaki' turns butter yellow. The full-moon maple, *Acer japonicum*, has leaves of basically rounded outline, though divided into lobes, whereas the Japanese maples are deeply fingered. The full-moon maple's two selections 'Aconitifolium' and 'Vitifolium' turn to rich shades of crimson and scarlet in the autumn. The golden full-moon maple, *A. shirasawanum* f. *aureum*, also turns scarlet, with an intermediate stage when each leaf displays both gold and scarlet.

In autumn, the flowering dogwood, *Cornus florida* 'Rainbow', starts to fulfil its name, turning from green and yellow to purple edged with red. Most of the cherries commended for their coloured spring foliage also colour up in autumn. One of the brightest is *Prunus sargentii*. A cherry relative which is in many respects

A single specimen of Japanese maple, Acer palmatum, *can make a tremendous impact in the right setting, where its intense autumn colours glow against a dark background.*

a better bet for small gardens is the snowy mespilus, *Amelanchier lamarckii*. Its buff and pink spring foliage was not quite colourful enough to earn it a place in Chapter 3, but its abundant, dainty white flowers are enchanting and its autumn tints outdo the cherries, in flame and scarlet.

Flowering and fruiting trees for autumn glory

Among the rowans, not only *Sorbus cashmeriana*, already extolled for its crimson-pink spring growths, but also many others, turn colour in autumn, displaying between them an extraordinary range of shades enhanced by white, pink, yellow, orange or scarlet berries. *S. cashmeriana* itself, which has white fruits, contrasts them with rich crimson and purple autumn foliage, while the pink- or white-fruited *S. hupehensis* favours dusky pink and purple, and dainty *S. vilmorinii*, with fruits that start rosy crimson and slowly fade through pink to white, has fine, frond-like foliage of similar crimson and purple colouring to *S. cashmeriana*. The rowans with orange or scarlet fruits display autumn foliage of similar tones, orange, scarlet and crimson; among the best are *S. scalaris* and *S. commixta*, while *S. sargentiana* also boasts fat, sticky winter buds after the scarlet leaves have fallen. There is a particular appeal to the contrasts shown by *S.* 'Joseph Rock', for its berries are soft yellow to amber, amid foliage that ranges from coral and orange through scarlet and crimson to purple.

Compared with the maples and rowans, crabs and thorns might seem rather unaristocratic. There are some fine things among them though, not just for spring flower but also for autumn foliage. My choice would be the crab that sounds like a sneeze, *Malus tschonoskii*, and the plum-leaved thorn, *Crataegus persimilis* 'Prunifolia'. The first is a medium-sized tree which turns to yellow, orange, scarlet and purple in autumn; the thorn is more fiery still in orange and scarlet.

A miscellany of autumn pyrotechnics

For many people, dogwood means the shrubs with bright winter stems and, if they think of the tree-like *Cornus controversa* at all, they mean its variegated form. Stunning though this is, the plain green form is also beautiful, with the same tabular, wedding-cake habit, a great froth of cream flowers in early summer and deep, dusky autumn tints of purple-red. If your neighbours already grow lots of maples, rowans and cherries, why not be different with this aristocratic tree? Another tree with a difference is *Cercidiphyllum japonicum*. In autumn the rounded leaves turn to shades of yellow or smoky pink and they smell intriguingly of hot toffee as they fall, the aroma carrying far on the air.

If your soil is suitable for rhododendrons – acid and leafy – you should also succeed with the stewartias, small trees with flowers like little white camellias (to which they are related), peeling, python-skin bark and rich autumn colours, red and gold in *Stewartia pseudocamellia* and red in *S. sinensis*.

The best possible canopy tree for rhododendrons is an oak, deep-rooting so it does not steal nutrients from the rhododendron's fibrous roots, and casting a friendly shade. You could start to make an oak canopy by planting one of the American oaks and, meanwhile, enjoy incandescent autumn colour, not to

Autumn leaves glow brightest with the light behind them. Adorning this pergola is Vitis coignetiae, *a vine from Japan.*

mention the bold, elegant patterns of the sharply lobed leaves all summer. The brightest is the scarlet oak, *Quercus coccinea*, which turns glowing, fiery scarlet. The leaves of the pin oak, *Q. palustris*, are slightly smaller but adopt the same fiery autumn tints; the red oak, *Q. rubra*, is a slightly more muted red.

If you have the space, it is worth including a tree that turns golden yellow in autumn, to set off all these brilliant reds. First choice would be a birch, with its silvery or apricot-pink bark, and smoky-purple winter twiggery. The silver birch, *Betula pendula*, is as fine an all-rounder as any and its leaves are smaller and daintier than many, pattering down in autumn like golden raindrops. For a stunning effect, plant a Virginia creeper (*Parthenocissus quinquefolia*), the coarser Boston ivy (*P. tricuspidata*), or even a *Vitis coignetiae*, where it can climb through the branches of a silver birch. Best of all, contrive to see it with the sun behind it, shining through the crimson and scarlet leaves, which will turn as translucent as coloured glass. Virginia creeper on a wall is beautiful; in a silver birch it is magical.

Mainly for bigger spaces

My last three trees are hardly recommended for small gardens, though if you have plenty of space they are fine things, if not truly double-value. The sweet gum, *Liquidambar styraciflua*, has maple-like leaves, pleasant but not particularly exciting until the autumn, when they colour brightly. Different trees turn different colours and some hardly perform at all; if you want to grow a sweet gum, it is worth choosing a seedling in its autumn garb or paying extra for a named variety such as 'Lane Roberts' or 'Worplesdon'. An old friend of mine with a big garden, some years ago decided to plant a grove of sweet gums, which he chose from their nursery rows, ending up with a rainbow of colour from pale lemon at one end, through coral and scarlet and crimson, to one tree so dark it was almost black.

Parrotia persica, like the sweet gum, is related to the witch hazels. It makes a wide, spreading bush, ultimately tree-like, with crimson and yellow autumn colouring. The black gum, or tupelo, *Nyssa sylvatica*, however, is no relation. The glossy leaves are very bright in autumn, scarlet, orange and yellow.

OFFBEAT FALL COLOURS –
THE AUTUMN GARDEN IN PINK AND PURPLE

A surprising number of autumn's flowers are in the pink to purple range – Michaelmas daisies, nerines and *Chrysanthemum* 'Emperor of China' (which has silvery-pink flowers amid deep crimson foliage) among them. There are shrubs that turn colour in this direction too. Let us suppose you chose to plant *Sorbus hupehensis* as the centrepiece of such a group. The next addition might be a callicarpa. *Callicarpa bodinieri* 'Profusion' astounds in autumn when its leaves turn to smoky purple and pink, amid clusters of berries of the most brilliant violet-magenta. The crimson-pink, mop-headed *Hydrangea* 'Preziosa' could join them, as much for its plum-purple and crimson foliage as its late flowers.

Most spindleberries flare up in bonfire colours but one, *Euonymus oxyphyllus*, quits the scene in rich ruby and purple. Better known are the lacecap viburnums, forms of *Viburnum plicatum*, a glory in late spring flower and again in autumn when they turn to red and plum purple. The variegated forms of *Berberis thunbergii*, especially the pale, cream and green 'Kelleris', lean towards pink autumn colouring rather than the scarlet of the plain green or purple forms. The same is true of the variegated fishbone cotoneaster, *C. horizontalis* 'Variegata', with its tiny, white-edged leaves; the dying leaves are pink, not scarlet. I have already mentioned the red-purple tones of the tree-like *Cornus controversa*; its stunning variegated form, 'Variegata', turns pink in autumn. *C. florida* 'Welchii' turns from green, pink and white to purple edged with rosy red.

If there is a wall nearby, the perfect climbing companion for this group would be *Parthenocissus henryana*, a cousin of the Virginia creeper with velvety, dark green leaves picked out with silver veins, turning to crimson and purple in autumn, when the white veins stand out still more clearly. The huge, dinner-plate leaves of *Vitis coignetiae* sometimes take on burnished-purple tones in autumn or flare up more brightly with scarlet and crimson amid the purple.

Amid the paler shades of pink and apricot, the amusing little double Chinese cherry, *Prunus glandulosa*, stands out in autumn. It is available in pink flower under the name 'Sinensis' or in white flower as 'Alba Plena'.

The spindle tree, Euonymus oxyphyllus, *has its moment of glory in autumn when the foliage takes on these rich tones.*

BONFIRE COLOURS FROM DUAL-SEASON SHRUBS

Even without a single tree in your garden, shrubberies and borders can turn incandescent as the nights draw in and the days grow colder. And, as with trees, a number of these shrubs have more to offer than just their autumn tints, making them excellent value for small gardens. When they are also happy in any reasonable soil, with no fears of lime, there can be no further hesitation.

Several forms of the Japanese *Acer palmatum* (see also page 71) never grow beyond shrub stature, especially the 'Dissectum' forms with their lacy-fine foliage in green, purple or deepest mahogany; they all flare up with just as much brilliance as their tree-sized cousins. The vine maple, *Acer circinatum*, is pretty in spring when bearing its claret and white flowers, and stunning in autumn when it turns to orange and crimson. The shrubby *Amelanchier canadensis* is much less particular than the Japanese maples and just as vivid in autumn as its more tree-like relative. It slowly spreads to form a many-stemmed, bulky shrub.

Like this amelanchier, the flowering dogwoods hover between shrub and tree status. *Cornus florida* is the North American species; the showy bracts that surround its tiny flowers in late spring are either white or pink and its autumn colour is uniformly bright in shades of scarlet, flame and rust. The Japanese *C. kousa* is better suited to maritime climates, where it colours just as vividly. If you have chalky soil, choose *C. kousa* var. *chinensis*. For all these dogwoods, improve the soil as much as you can with leaf mould or garden compost.

The witch hazels like similar conditions. *Hamamelis vernalis* 'Sandra' (see Chapter 3) puts on a firework display in autumn when the rounded leaves turn to orange, scarlet and crimson. The yellow-flowered witch hazels, *H. mollis* and *H. japonica*, with their spidery, scented winter flowers, mostly turn yellow but the hybrid between the two ranges in flower colour from lemon-primrose to blood red, with the autumn leaf colour roughly correlated; thus 'Moonlight' turns yellow, the foliage of orange 'Jelena' dies off in shades of orange, red and scarlet, and deep red 'Diane' is richly coloured in the scarlet to red range.

Few barberries are as aristocratic as the witch hazels, and we have already met *Berberis thunbergii* in several of its manifestations as a colourful foliage shrub for summer (Chapter 4). Without exception, they colour brightly in autumn, usually to shades of scarlet and crimson, though *B. thunbergii* 'Aurea' is orange rather than red. The real gem among autumn-tinted barberries is *B. dictyophylla*, a year-rounder if ever there was one. It has blue-glaucous foliage, large (for a berberis) lemon-yellow flowers, the most intense crimson-scarlet autumn colouring very late in the season and, when at last the leaves finally drop, the white-washed winter stems are fully revealed.

Like so many *Berberis thunbergii* variants, *Cotinus coggygria* is often chosen for its purple foliage but both green and purple forms are dramatic in autumn, with their scarlet and crimson colouring. 'Flame' has been specially selected for the brightness of its scarlet dying leaves. *C. obovatus* is bigger in stature and in leaf, and every bit as brilliant in autumn.

One of the most unusual hydrangeas is the oak-leaved *Hydrangea quercifolia*; the oak it is named for is not the English oak, with its smallish, round-lobed leaves,

Although its flowers cannot quite compete with the winter-flowering witch hazel, Hamamelis vernalis *'Sandra' is an all-rounder with richly-tinted spring foliage and brilliant autumn tones.*

but the American *Quercus coccinea*, with big, bold, pointed lobes. The hydrangea bears cone-shaped, lacy, white panicles of flower, followed by rich autumn tints of scarlet, crimson and russet. The sumach, *Rhus typhina*, is hardly equalled in autumn when the ample fronds turn orange, scarlet and red.

How many of us think of roses for autumn colour, I wonder? Yet there are some that hold their own against any shrub claiming the right to inclusion for its bright tints. *Rosa virginiana*, which has single, pink flowers and glossy, green foliage, turns orange and scarlet, while the smaller, also pink-flowered *R. nitida* has even more highly polished foliage that dies off in vibrant shades of scarlet and crimson before falling to reveal red winter stems. To contrast with all this red, *R. rugosa*, with its sumptuous, silky, fragrant flowers in white, pink or magenta, single or double, has leathery, ribbed leaves that turn corn gold in the fall.

Winter stems of bright orange-red qualify *Cornus sanguinea* 'Winter Beauty' (also known as 'Winter Flame') for inclusion with the dual-season shrubs. Unusually, its autumn foliage shows warm shades of orange and flame.

ONE-SHOT SHRUBS AND CLIMBERS

As well as dual-season plants, there are those that put all their efforts into a single season of glory – autumn. The form of the Tatarian maple known as *Acer tataricum* ssp. *ginnala* (syn. *A. ginnala*) is quite a pretty foliage plant in summer but, judged in this season alone, it cannot compare with the Japanese maples. However, it redeems itself in autumn when it is vivid orange, crimson and scarlet.

The winged spindle, Euonymus alatus, *is one of the first shrubs to colour in autumn.*

The chokeberries are related to the rowans but look very different, forming rather upright shrubs with unremarkable white flowers followed, in autumn, by bright red fruits in *Aronia arbutifolia*, the red chokeberry, and black, glossy berries in the black chokeberry, *A. melanocarpa*. In both, the fruits are set off by foliage of incandescent brilliance, shading from orange to scarlet.

Fruit and foliage, again, create the autumn effect of the spindleberry, *Euonymus planipes*, blending scarlet and flame foliage and large, scarlet fruits. *E. alatus* only goes in for foliage, colouring – and falling – very early in the season at the start of the autumn display.

Autumn foliage does not have to turn uniformly scarlet or gold to appeal. Part of the attraction of *Vitis* 'Brant', apart from its dark, sweet, aromatic grapes, is the way in which the boldly lobed leaves turn crimson and purple with the veins retaining their green colouring in striking contrast. It is tough and hardy and will grow through a host tree, or grace a pergola, in classic style.

AUTUMN COLOUR FROM CONIFERS

There are a few deciduous conifers that colour up in the fall as their foliage dies away. One of them is not at all like our image of a conifer, for it has leaves like a vastly magnified maidenhair fern. I refer, of course, to the maidenhair tree, *Ginkgo biloba*, sole survivor from a far distant era 160 million years or more ago. Its autumn foliage is an attractive clear yellow.

The swamp cypress, *Taxodium distichum*, is a symmetrical pyramid of a tree with fresh, soft-green needles that turn orange, tan and bronze in autumn. The dawn cypress, *Metasequoia glyptostroboïdes*, is like a larger, coarser version of the swamp cypress, with similar orange and tawny-pink autumn tints.

Only for gardens with acid soil, Disanthus cercidifolius *is a shrub of great distinction, with some of the richest autumn tints of the season.*

AUTUMN TINTS AMONG THE RHODODENDRONS

In gardens blessed with acid soil, the evergreen foliage of rhododendrons is the ideal foil for lime-hating plants that lose their leaves in a blaze of colour in autumn. One of the finest is the sorrel tree, *Oxydendrum arboreum*, a large shrub with sprays of white flowers in summer, after virtually all the rhododendrons are long over, and scintillating autumn colour of orange, scarlet and crimson. Many deciduous azaleas also display rich autumn tints; among the best, though it needs plenty of room, is the honeysuckle azalea, *R. luteum*.

Enkianthus campanulatus is the best known of a genus related to rhododendrons and needing similar conditions. With their open habit of growth, small leaves and abundant, tiny, bell-shaped flowers ranging from white through coral to deep red, they would be valued even without their autumn tints of orange, scarlet and crimson. Any enkianthus you see is worth buying, but *E. perulatus* is specially worth a mention for its consistently vivid, pure scarlet autumn foliage.

In contrast to the airy enkianthuses, the fothergillas are solid-looking, with ivory-white, bottlebrush flowers in spring and rounded leaves that colour to scarlet and orange in autumn. The smaller species is *Fothergilla gardenii*, while *F. major*, which has glaucous-backed leaves, now includes *F. monticola*. Desirable though they are, the fothergillas cannot hold a candle to *Disanthus cercidifolius*. As its name suggests, it is a plant with leaves like a Judas tree but twice the size and of the richest, most glowing ruby crimson and purple in autumn.

Most eucryphias are evergreen but there is one deciduous species, *Eucryphia glutinosa*, that makes a large shrub or small, bushy tree, which, in late summer, is decked with white, saucer-shaped flowers, each filled with the brush of stamens

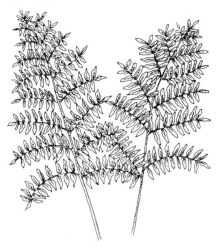

Fig 14 *The royal fern,* Osmunda regalis, *is indeed one of the noblest of hardy ferns, with its large, upstanding fronds, that turn to copper and orange in autumn.*

typical of eucryphias; these lie amid pinnate leaves that, in autumn, go out in a blaze of crimson, scarlet and flame.

A noble companion for rhododendrons and their autumn-colouring companions is the royal fern, *Osmunda regalis*, a mass of elegant greenery in summer turning to yellow and bronze in autumn.

AUTUMN COLOUR IN THE FLOWER BORDER

Aruncus aethusifolius, with its pretty apricot tints, is one of the few perennials that puts on any sort of autumn foliage display. Many hostas turn deep gold, Solomon's seal fades to paler gold and parchment, paeonies often die away in shades of orange and flame, and the small plumbagos, *Ceratostigma plumbaginoïdes* and the subshrubby *C. willmottianum* and *C. griffithii*, bear their ultramarine-blue flowers amid the scarlet and crimson of their autumn foliage. The strongly aromatic *Geranium macrorrhizum* often shows scarlet and red dying leaves amid the green.

Many grasses slowly fade from their summer green or variegated tints to shades of parchment that, if not beaten down by the weather, last through the winter. Far more attractive than these dead leaves, in autumn, is *Miscanthus sinensis* var. *purpurascens*, which deepens to madder-brown with pink central veins by late summer, only to turn red, orange and buff in the autumn.

Until the selection 'Chameleon' was introduced, *Euphorbia dulcis* was not much valued, despite its astonishing autumn tints, rivalling any shrub in flame, orange and scarlet. 'Chameleon' is not only velvety purple in spring and summer, as we have seen, but is the equal of its plain green parent in its autumn garb.

Annuals are so much associated with bright summer flowers that it is easy to forget the burning bush, *Kochia scoparia* f. *trichophylla*, a column of feathery green or purple in summer that turns to fiery red in autumn.

CHAPTER 7

FOLIAGE IN WINTER

AFTER THE FLARING foliage tints of autumn, winter is a quiet season, a season for the enjoyment of subtler pleasures. When not blanketed by snow, the garden in winter is still full of colour, mainly muted but warm and reassuring amid the frosts or under the low, pale sun.

If you want to reinforce the impression of coldness, to point up the contrast with golden or burgundy-red foliage, choose plants with blue-grey foliage; some plants of this colouring deepen to steely tones with the cold, while others remain pale and aloof of complexion. For an illusion of warmth, there are the evergreens that flush crimson, mahogany or burgundy-purple with the cold, and the yellow-variegated evergreens that really come into their own at this season.

CONIFERS IN WINTER

Several cultivars of *Juniperus horizontalis*, among the flattest of carpeters, turn bronze or purple with the cold; one of the best is 'Wiltonii', glaucous blue in summer and steely purple in winter. Warmer colours belong to the ever-popular *Thuja occidentalis* 'Rheingold', a fluffy bun of a plant that turns to coppery gold and amber in winter, and to the dwarf pine, *Pinus mugo* 'Ophir', which is bright golden yellow in the cold months. Other conifers turn purple, fox red or bronze. *Thuja orientalis* 'Meldensis' is plum purple in winter and the very similar 'Rosedalis', also a feathery, small mound, has glaucous overtones to its burgundy winter garb. The taller 'Juniperoïdes' turns almost mauve with the frosts. *Chamaecyparis thyoïdes* 'Ericoides' is another small, needle-leaved conifer that turns bronze and wine red with the cold. 'Rubicon' is similar but smaller and redder. There are two diminutive forms of the Japanese cedar, *Cryptomeria japonica*, which turn from dark green to fox red and purple in winter: 'Compressa', and 'Vilmoriniana'.

You need more space for *Cryptomeria japonica* 'Elegans', well-named for its cloudy masses of foliage, green in summer turning to russet and bronze-purple in winter. 'Elegans Compacta', in rich purple, is smaller but still no dwarf. Both have a maddening tendency to fall over or splay open if weighed down by snow.

The golden Scots pine, *Pinus sylvestris* 'Aurea', is bright yellow in winter and a better colour than the golden Christmas tree, *Picea abies* 'Aurea', which is rather dull, though its neat formal shape commends it. The golden Monterey pine, *P.*

This Juniperus x media *'Pfitzeriana' has been pruned to make a low, flat umbrella of foliage above silvery* Santolina chamaecyparissus, *both of them white with frost on a winter's day.*

radiata 'Aurea', is promising, with the same ample clusters of needles as its plain green relative but of the most vivid yellow in winter. By contrast, *Chamaecyparis pisifera* 'Squarrosa Sulphurea' is as pale as winter sunshine when its greyish-sulphur, feathery foliage fades to cream, just touched with warming, bronze tints.

WINTER COLOUR ON ACID SOILS

Gardeners with lime-free soils can grow the full range of heaths and heathers that are at their most vivid in the cold weather. The bright orange and red winter tints that we seek for their cheering qualities work best in small quantities amid other acid-loving shrubs; they are very potent, even under the grey skies of winter. If you want them in larger sweeps, the deliberate artificiality of abstract patterns could be the answer.

Forms of *Calluna vulgaris*, above all, are bonfire-bright, as some of their names suggest: 'Blazeaway' in rich red, 'Firefly' nearer to orange, 'Wickwar Flame' in orange deepening to scarlet. 'Sunset' is quieter, in orange-gold turning bronze with the cold; 'Winter Chocolate' is another of muted tones. 'Sir John Charrington' and 'Robert Chapman' in gold turning to flame and scarlet – the first taller than average, the second unusually compact and dense – and 'Joy Vanstone' in rich orange, are just as heart-warming in the frosty months. 'Golden Feather' is warm orange in winter. Several other callunas are yellow all year: 'Beoley Gold', compact 'Golden Carpet', which takes on warmer, if not exactly orange, tints in winter, and the taller 'Serlei Aurea' and 'Gold Haze'. Among the ericas there are fewer winter pyrotechnics, but *Erica cinerea* 'Golden Hue' and 'Windlebrooke' emulate the callunas in their tones of yellow deepening to orange and red.

If you prefer a more informal look, there are a number of broad-leaved evergreens that demand the same acid soils as the callunas. The evergreen foliage of the wintergreen, *Gaultheria procumbens*, turns mahogany red in winter. This lowly carpeter, which also decks itself with scarlet berries, prefers a moist soil, as does another red-berried small relative, the cowberry, *Vaccinium vitis-idaea*, burnished copper in winter. The leucothoës add height to a grouping on acid soil. *L. fontanesiana* is the better known; its arching stems set with leathery leaves turning to copper and beetroot purple in winter. The smaller *L. keiskei* has zigzag stems and smaller leaves but is no less richly tinted with the cold.

Remember that, to colour up in this way, they need plenty of light; to compensate for summer heat, make sure the soil is leafy and cool. The same conditions will suit the rhododendrons known as PJM hybrids, which turn red and purple in winter. Many evergreen azaleas, grown above all for their spring flowers, also colour in winter, taking on shades of crimson and burgundy.

Most perennials are lime-tolerant but there is one for the winter garden that insists on acid soil: *Galax urceolata* (syn. *G. aphylla*). Reaching about 30 cm (12 in), it has almost circular, leathery leaves on wiry stems; their glossy finish is enhanced by the mahogany and beetroot winter colouring.

WINTER FOLIAGE FOR ALKALINE SOILS

The only heaths that are properly lime-tolerant are *Erica carnea*, its hybrid *E. × darleyensis* and, the other parent of the cross, *E. erigena* (syn. *E. mediterranea*). There are a few cultivars with golden foliage all year round, among them *E. × darleyensis* 'Jack H. Brummage', a 45 cm (18 in) mound with bright yellow leaves and pink winter flowers. *E. carnea* 'Foxhollow' is an unusual shade of yellow flushed with pink and red.

Several of the mahonias colour richly with the onset of winter, from the familiar Oregon grape, *M. aquifolium*, to its scarce hybrids *M. × wagneri* 'Undulata', with narrow, glossy leaves turning mahogany-purple in the cold, and the extraordinary 'Moseri' that changes all year, from bronze-red in spring to apple green in summer to scarlet, orange and flame in winter. These grow to 90 cm (3 ft) or so but *M. nervosa* is half the height and very decorative with its hard-textured leaves, disposed along the stems in a striking pattern, heightened by the burnished-copper winter colour. Even the well-known *M. japonica*, if grown in full exposure to sun and wind, in a light, hungry soil, will take on shades of coral and peach in winter.

The climbing *Euonymus fortunei* 'Coloratus' – which makes splendid ground-cover if grown on the flat – has green leaves in summer but, with the cold, turns blood red. Some of the ivies, too, colour up in winter: *Hedera helix* 'Glymii' is almost black, a wonderful contrast to snowdrops or the first primroses; and 'Tricolor', cream, pink and green in summer, adds blackcurrant purple to its cold-weather repertoire. Like the euonymus, these ivies can of course be grown as climbers or on the flat.

Except in virtually frost-free climates, it is wise to give *Trachelospermum jasminoïdes* 'Variegatum' the protection of a wall to grow on; it is fairly hardy, but far too pretty to risk losing, with its cream-variegated, pink-touched foliage that turns to rich crimson and rose in winter. This is a plant with star quality, fit to grow around your front door to give year-round pleasure and with the bonus of deliciously fragrant flowers in summer.

PERENNIALS THAT COLOUR IN WINTER

The bold, leathery leaves of many bergenias change from green to shades of mahogany, crimson, burgundy and liver, provided that they are grown in sunny places. Miss Jekyll's favourite, *B. cordifolia* 'Purpurea', has very large leaves turning purplish, and another popular old kind, *B. crassifolia*, develops mahogany tones. Some hybrid bergenias also colour well: 'Sunningdale', bronze-purple backed with mahogany red; 'Abendglut' in plum red; and 'Ballawley', with large leaves turning mahogany purple. *B. purpurascens* holds its rather narrow, spoon-shaped leaves upright; they turn beetroot purple, backed with red, in winter and form a striking contrast to the ivory and green spears of *Iris foetidissima* 'Variegata'. Add the old-gold, conifer-like *Hebe ochracea* 'James Stirling', and you have a year-round group of form and colour that will really come into its own in winter.

The leathery leaves of Bergenia purpurascens *turn to deep liver and mahogany tones in winter.*

Fig 15 Bergenia purpurascens *is smaller in leaf than many bergenias; as a foliage plant it comes into its own in winter.*

The dark sea-green foliage of the shrubby euphorbias, *E. characias* and its close ally *E. characias* spp. *wulfenii*, often flushes purplish in winter. At least one seedling has been selected and propagated for this quality; its name, 'Perry's Winter Blusher', suggests something paler than the rich maroon and burgundy tones it adopts as the cold weather arrives. More reddish tones come from *Tellima grandiflora* Rubra Group, which colours even in shade, though more intensely if growing in full light. *Rubra*, of course, means 'red', and the winter colouring of the tellima's hairy, vine-shaped leaves is crimson and burgundy. The related tiarellas are more restrained, taking on bronzed tones. The heucheras are also related; one of the best for winter effect is *Heuchera* 'Taff's Joy', with densely cream-flecked leaves blushing pink and the deepest, richest tones at the margin. With all these broad, lobed leaves, a contrast of form as well as colour is called for. In mild climates the libertias are popular because of their brilliant white, three-cornered flowers. In winter the narrow sword leaves of both *L. ixioïdes* and the smaller *L. peregrinans* turn to orange.

If you want winter colour in a shady place, it is no good planting bergenias; they will stay resolutely green. But the variegated *Iris foetidissima* is just as good in shade as in sun. Another first-rate shade plant is *Arum italicum* var. *pictum*, which is winter-green and summer-deciduous – though, in summer, after the leaves fade, it does leave behind showy spikes of glossy, orange berries. In winter the arrow-head leaves unfurl, bold and green with conspicuous white veining.

WINTER BEDDING AND CONTAINERS

Even in the most permanent of plantings, there may be gaps in winter which you would like to fill with colour. For this role there is nothing better than the ornamental cabbages and kales, which look equally good massed or in small groups. Given space, you can use their different but harmonizing colours – ivory white, pink, magenta and purple – in combination to make more of those tropically inspired curls and spirals. These cabbages do just as well in containers;

There is no need for containers to be dull in winter. Here, ornamental cabbages nestle among variegated ivy, Euonymus fortunei *and* Skimmia japonica.

there is no need for those pots or tubs, so full of colour and interest in summer, to be empty in winter. Each plant, well-grown, can reach 45 cm (18 in) across, and their frilly outer leaves give an attractive finish to the container.

Many of the conifers already described do well in containers and those that change colour with the seasons are ideal for confounding those people who regard conifers as boringly the same all year. It is worth choosing attractive containers – terracotta or stone rather than plastic – to set them off. Increasingly, conifers are used in window boxes too, for winter display, with variegated ivies, well-budded specimens of *Skimmia japonica* 'Rubella', young plants of purple or variegated cordylines or pot-grown primroses; the permutations are many and the effects endlessly variable. If you have a deep pocket, you can buy specimen conifers already grown to a reasonable size; the more dwarf and slower-growing the variety, the more expensive they will be if you want instant effects. The faster-growing varieties can spend a season or two in a container, or a single winter in a window box, before you plant them in the garden in their permanent site; slower kinds may last for years before you feel the need to plant them out.

Conifers in containers are more vulnerable to the stress of drought, wind or cold than if they are growing in beds and borders among other plants. Be sure to keep them well watered in summer and spray the foliage daily during hot, dry spells. They can suffer from cold-induced drought in winter, when the roots cannot draw sufficient moisture from the cold or frozen soil to compensate for the water loss caused by chill winds or a sudden warm, sunny winter's day. It can help to spray container-grown conifers with anti-desiccant in early winter. In very cold spells, move them into a sheltered place and, if necessary, wrap the containers to protect the roots against alternate freezing and thawing.

CHAPTER 8

ARCHITECTURAL FOLIAGE PLANTS

ARCHITECTURAL PLANTS ARE those that draw the eye by their strong outlines and striking foliage. Such plants, ideally, should be evergreens, contributing year-round to the architecture of the garden. A plant that loses its leaves may be 'architectural' in its season – think of the cardoon (*Cynara cardunculus*), for example, with its great, jagged, silvery-grey leaves – but only the most exceptional will rate a mention here.

There is, of course, a snag to concentrating on evergreens. Some of the most spectacular of architectural plants are not very frost-resistant. The sort of plants I have in mind are agaves, opuntias, coloured phormiums and the like. Even if your climate is not benign enough for them to survive outdoors, you may be able to

Fig 16 *The cardoon,* Cynara cardunculus, *with its huge thistle-like leaves of brightest silver, is another old-fashioned vegetable (like seakale) that makes a superb foliage plant.*

grow them. Increasingly, gardeners are growing plants in containers and some of these dramatic plants are ideal for this purpose. If you can move them into shelter during the winter, you can at least enjoy them during the summer months; if that shelter is a conservatory, you can enjoy them all year round. Indoors or out, they are too good to omit from these pages.

Because they are so striking, architectural plants impose themselves wherever they grow. You can create a desert ambience with yuccas, agaves and succulents amid gravel and rocks, or associate them with mimosas (*Acacia*), eucalypts, the blue hesper palm and silver-leaved plants for a Mediterranean or Californian-style garden. You can dream up a lush jungle with aralias, fatsias and the huge, rubber-plant leaves of *Magnolia delavayi*. Or you can use a single architectural plant in a carefully composed picture to draw the eye, to act as a focal point.

SWORDS AND SPEARS

The simple, bold outline of sword-shaped leaves is especially compelling in contrast to rounded outlines or feathery, ferny foliage. Among the most valuable of 'spikies' are the yuccas and, of the hardy species, the most imposing is *Yucca gloriosa*, with its fiercely needle-pointed leaves forming bold rosettes. For year-round colour as well as form, its primrose-striped form 'Variegata' is a must.

Lesser variegated yuccas include *Y. flaccida* 'Golden Sword', with shorter, less rigidly stiff leaves brightly variegated with yellow, and *Y. filamentosa* 'Bright Edge' and 'Variegata', smaller again and less loud than 'Golden Sword'. Though most yuccas will form a stem in time (and some of the more tender species grow tall and branched), *Y. filamentosa* is always stemless, increasing by offsets so you get a slowly spreading patch of rosettes of striped or plain, arching sword leaves characterized by the curling threads along the margins. It will get knocked back by a severe winter, but bobs up again provided that the roots do not freeze.

Outstanding among yuccas is *Y. whipplei*, which has narrow, rapier leaves, up to 90 cm (3 ft) long and fiercely sharp at the tips, of intense blue-grey, arranged in a hemispherical rosette. Unlike the easy-going yuccas just described, it must have sharp drainage and full sun, not just to look its best but to survive.

Though the shape of the leaves in the New Zealand flaxes or phormiums and yuccas is similar, their arrangement is different. Instead of a rosette of sword or rapier leaves radiating from a central point, the blades of phormiums are arranged in fan-like fashion in a single plane.

There are two basic phormiums: *Phormium tenax*, with tall fans of stiff sword leaves up to 1.8 m (6 ft) long, and the smaller *P. cookianum*, in which the leaves are more lax and arch gracefully. There are phormiums of green and yellow or green and primrose colouring: *P. tenax* 'Variegatum' has narrow cream margins to the leaf. 'Yellow Wave' has stiff leaves up to 1.2 m (4 ft) long, striped with yellow; 'Cream Delight' is a form of *P. cookianum* growing to 90 cm (3 ft), with creamy-yellow stripes along its arching blades.

Opposite: *Spiky plants bring an alien, yet welcome note to the garden, with their hint of hotter climates. Here, variegated yuccas combine with a succulent agave to suggest a desert garden.*

Phormium tenax also comes in an imposing purple form, 'Purpureum', 1.5 m (5 ft) or more in height, with leaves of a bloomy, bronze-purple colour. If this is too massive, there are smaller versions available, ranging from 'Dark Delight' in rich oxblood-purple, through 'Bronze Baby', to little 'Thumbelina', a mere 30 cm (12 in) of dark purple rapier leaves, fit only to dominate a trough.

If it is colour you want, however, phormiums go much further, with a range of crushed raspberry, coral, sunset, apricot, amber, chocolate and bronze tones. The old *P. cookianum* 'Tricolor' is by far the quietest, little more than cream on green stripes with a narrow red margin. 'Sundowner' has stiff leaves up to 1.8 m (6 ft) long, striped with rose, apricot, bronze and chocolate. The others mainly have arching sword leaves: 'Dazzler' is chocolate and blood red, striped with rose, and the Maori series run to rose, coral, tan and bronze. It has to be said that the more colourful a phormium, the less frost-resistant it is.

In time the various species of cordyline make woody trunks, crowned with great tufts of rapier leaves. In youth, before the trunks start to grow, the leaves form symmetrical rosettes. The New Zealand cabbage tree, *Cordyline australis*, is popular in its purple forms. Often seed-raised, these vary from milk chocolate to deepest oxblood red; 'Torbay Red' is a named variety chosen for its outstanding colouring. There are also variegated cordylines: 'Albertii' with white and red stripes on green, and the newer, smart cream and green 'Torbay Dazzler'. 'Sundance' has a crimson centre. Only for frost-free regions are the even more colourful forms of *C. fruticosa* (syn. *C. stricta*) the ti.

Astelia nervosa var. *chathamica* 'Silver Spear' makes bold, silver-grey rosettes of wide, spear-shaped leaves. There are lesser astelias too, all worth snapping up though they are not so silvery in leaf. If knocked back by frost they usually recover, though not if the roots are frozen.

Most red hot pokers are valued for their showy flower spikes but a few are handsome foliage plants as well. The most familiar is *Kniphofia caulescens*, which produces thick stems that lie about on the ground like discarded elephants' trunks, from which arise rosettes of blue-grey, sword-shaped leaves. It is evergreen, though apt to look a touch miserable in chilly, wet winters.

'Broadsword' best describes the leaf shape of *Beschorneria yuccoïdes*, an extraordinary Mexican native related to agaves. It produces massive rosettes of blue-grey leaves, slowly spreading by offsets. Handsome in themselves, when the plant comes into flower they form the perfect designer-plinth for the wrist-thick, rhubarb-red flowering stems topped by nodding, coral and green bells.

Spiky xerophytes

Since we have come to agave relatives, it seems a good moment to describe the agaves themselves. Those that I shall mention will withstand a little frost but particularly dislike the combination of cold and wet; they are semi-succulent, designed to withstand longish periods of drought (xerophytes are plants adapted to dry conditions). One of the toughest is *Agave americana*, which makes bold rosettes of broad-based, grey-blue leaves, armed at the margins and tips with sharp spines. It has some spectacular variegated forms: 'Marginata' with creamy-yellow

Fig 17 *Before it has developed a distinct trunk, a youthful plant of* Cordyline australis *'Albertii' is reminiscent of a firework, with its star-burst of striped, sword-shaped leaves.*

margins; 'Mediopicta' with creamy white at the centre; and 'Variegata' with yellow central variegation. The massive rosettes of *A. franzosinii* are intensely silvery blue, with curving leaves.

The spines of these agaves are as nothing compared with the ferocious shark's teeth hooks that beset the leaves of fascicularias and puyas. These South American semi-succulents are surprisingly hardy and wonderfully alien-looking. The

Whereas yuccas form rosettes of rapier-like leaves, phormiums bear their broad-sword leaves in fans, stiff in Phormium tenax *and gracefully arching in* P. cookianum *and its derivatives.*

fascicularias are the smaller in growth, both *Fascicularia bicolor* and *F. pitcairniifolia* (the larger of the two) forming slowly spreading colonies of narrow, grey-green leaves with paler reverse. The flowers are rounded, stemless clusters of pale blue at the centre of the leaf rosettes, which turn vivid scarlet as the flowers open and fade as the flowers themselves go over.

There are several puyas, some of them monsters needing a lot of space if you plan to grow them in the open ground. One of the more manageable is *Puya alpestris*, which makes bolder, grey-green rosettes than the fascicularias but every bit as fiercely armed. The flowers, borne on a spike, are an astonishing electric blue. Although they look so exotic, puyas are surprisingly easy to tame in a container, though you will need to handle them with care and thick gloves.

SMALL BUT STRIKING

The most telling way to show off your big, bold spikies is often to spread a lowly carpet around them, so nothing interferes, visually, with their characteristic outline. There is no reason, however, why these smaller companions should not themselves be endowed with strong lines. Take, for example, *Euphorbia myrsinites*. The trailing stems of this small, evergreen spurge are set with pointed leaves of bright glaucous blue, disposed on the stems in a way that calls to mind a branchlet of a monkey puzzle tree (*Araucaria araucana*) that someone has dipped in silver paint. The rather similar *E. rigida* has leaves of the same colouring but set in a less rigidly geometric fashion on the more upright stems. The same blue-grey tones occur again in *Othonna cheirifolia*, another evergreen with spoon-shaped leaves packed into tight, barely unfurled fans on sprawling stems.

The larger houseleeks, forms of *Sempervivum tectorum*, range in colour from green to deep burgundy, through green tipped with red, chocolate and bronze. The formal design of their fleshy rosettes is enhanced by their mode of growth, slowly spreading to form what Beth Chatto has evocatively likened to a mosaic paving. In mild-winter areas you can spread carpets of blue, white-mealed or mauve-flushed echeveria rosettes instead, or the intensely white-leaved *Dudleya farinosa*, which looks much like an echeveria.

Fleshy rosettes are also found in *Aeonium arboreum* though this, as its name implies, grows stems rather than making a flat carpet. Each succulent leaf is blunt-ended and broader at the tip than the base. The type has green leaves and is completely outshone by 'Atropurpureum', in which the rosettes are polished mahogany-purple, and by the black-purple 'Zwartkop'. They are superb when set in a sea of *Calocephalus brownii*, an Australian ever-silver with stems that look like tangled, platinum wire.

With the plant that most of us still call *Setcreasea purpurea* (*Tradescantia pallida*) I am on shakier ground, for its fleshy, pointed leaves, very like those of tradescantias (which is what we are now supposed to call the setcreasea), are remarkable mainly for their extraordinary violet-purple colouring, faintly sheened with silver. It spreads on prostrate stems and is the perfect carpeting companion for a blue or variegated yucca or agave. Surprisingly hardy once established, it will usually grow again from below ground if cut by frost.

Fig 18 *A well-grown* Fatsia japonica *plant may have leaves 30cm (12in) or more across, of bright glossy green, the margin of each 'finger' seductively waved and crimped. It thrives in shady gardens.*

One of the hardiest of opuntias, the Utah grizzly bear opuntia (*O. erinacea* var. *utahensis*) has short, upright branches arising from a spreading, prostrate mat; some forms, known as *O. rhodanthe*, flush with purple when grown in full sun. Perhaps it is cheating to include opuntias, since they have nothing that a more conventional plant would recognize as foliage, the fleshy pads doing the work normally performed by leaves.

THE BEST AND BOLDEST LEAVES

For bold foliage you can hardly beat *Fatsia japonica*, often grown as a house plant but every bit as valuable outdoors, especially in town gardens where its strong outline and great, palmate leaves hold their own against the hard lines of traditional and modern architecture alike. Each lobe of the dark, glossy leaves is seductively wavy at the margins. There is a variegated form which is so understated you scarcely notice the cream margins. Less hardy than the fatsia is the Japanese rice paper plant, *Tetrapanax papyrifer*. The leaves are also large and palmate, but the effect is rather different, with broad, sharply cut lobes instead of undulating fingers, of greyish tone with silvery white or russet reverse.

A mild, if not wholly frost–free climate is also the recipe for success outdoors with *Pseudopanax lessonii* 'Gold Splash', which in these conditions will grow to 3 m (10 ft) or more, but can be grown in a container in colder regions. The waxy, polished leaves are composed of three to five bold leaflets, broadest near the tip and marked at the centre with bright daffodil yellow. 'Purpureus' has the same leaf outline and waxy texture but in metallic purple.

The silvery New Zealand shrubby senecios, now classified as *Brachyglottis*, are a diverse lot. One of the more tender is *B. repanda*, its large, slightly lobed leaves

Fig 19 *The large leaves of* Brachyglottis repanda *'Purpurea' are easily torn by the wind, so it is worth finding a sheltered place where their unusual combination of glossy, purple-black upper surface and white-felted reverse can be enjoyed in unspoilt perfection.*

textured like thin leather, polished on one side and suede-finished on the other. The general effect is greyish but, in 'Purpurea' the white reverse is allied to an upper surface of glossy black–purple. It needs wind shelter to prevent the leaves from tearing.

The South African *Melianthus major* is also happiest in a mild climate but it does have the obliging ability to behave like a herbaceous plant; if its woody tops are killed by frost, new shoots will grow from below ground provided that the roots themselves are not frozen. Its leaves are so stunningly beautiful that it is worth every care; the best leaves, anyway, appear on plants that have been cut back in spring, so if the frost does not do the job, your secateurs should. Each large frond is composed of several broad leaflets with saw-toothed margins, giving an overall effect of some huge, glaucous blue feather; on first unfurling, these lovely plumes are pale jade green and primrose.

Palm trees certainly deserve to be described as architectural but most are green. Few ally form and colour so successfully as the Mexican blue hesper palm or grey goddess, *Brahea armata*. Ultimately reaching 9 m (30 ft), it bears waxy, stiff fans of blue-grey foliage. The California fan palm, *Washingtonia filifera*, can grow considerably taller, but at all stages is handsome with its almost circular, deeply pleated fans of grey-green leaves margined with hairy threads. Neither is suited to cold climates, though they will take a little frost.

Many acacias have attractive foliage, though perhaps it is stretching the definition a little far to call them architectural. One that does, I think, qualify is *Acacia pravissima*, a small tree with slender, weeping branches closely set with triangular, blue-green 'phyllodes' (stems modified to do the work of leaves). *A.*

podalyriifolia, the Queensland silver wattle, has wedge-shaped phyllodes, much larger and intensely glaucous with a covering of fine white down.

In complete contrast to these are the massive, plain leaves of *Magnolia delavayi*, which resemble nothing so much as those of the rubber plant (*Ficus elastica*) so familiar as a house plant. The magnolia is slightly tender but will grow reasonably well with wall protection in climates like that of southern England, and makes a noble tree in the south-west of the UK or in equivalent mild, moist regions. Each great leaf is dark sea-green in colour with a soft, grape-like bloom. The tougher bull bay, *M. grandiflora*, has smaller leaves of glossier, brighter green, backed in some forms with russet felt.

SEASONAL ARCHITECTURE

There are a few deciduous trees so exceptional when in leaf that they have to find a place here even if their winter effect is negligible or zero. First is *Cornus controversa* 'Variegata'. A specimen old enough to have developed its characteristic

No wonder Cornus controversa *'Variegata' is nicknamed the wedding cake tree.*

tiered, wedding-cake habit is like nothing else when decked with its abundant, white-variegated leaves. By contrast the more shrubby *C. alternifolia* 'Argentea', which also develops a tiered habit but more often around several main stems, has foliage so delicate that the shrub seems hardly to be earth-bound.

There are two variegated forms of the Japanese angelica tree, *Aralia elata*. Both have the same immense, bipinnate leaves (that is, with leaflets arising from side stems of the main stem). In spring the two are quite distinct, 'Aureovariegata' margined yellow and 'Variegata' edged with white, but, as spring passes into summer, the yellow of the first fades to cream until it is virtually impossible to tell them apart. At all times when in leaf, however, they are superb.

ARCHITECTURAL BEDDING

This is another kind of seasonal effect; not one that comes and goes with the seasons, but one that you yourself can choose for a season and then discard. As happens so often, the plants we use for this purpose may in fact be perennials or even shrubs in frost-free climates. So it is with the castor oil plant, *Ricinus communis*. The largest and most striking foliage, however, is borne by well-grown first-year seedlings: big, palmate leaves up to 30 cm (12 in) across, most exciting in their coloured manifestations such as metallic-purple 'Gibsonii', plum-red 'Carmencita' or the bronze-green 'Impala', which has bright red stems.

The variegated corn, *Zea mays* 'Quadricolor', has wide, arching blades striped pink, red and cream on green, making a vivid fountain of colour to soar above lesser plants in your bedding schemes. Plants such as cannas, already described in Chapter 5, have an architectural quality thanks to their great paddle-shaped leaves, and are well adapted to seasonal bedding.

BIZARRE AND BEAUTIFUL

Here are a few real oddities for your delectation. First, two prickly pears. *Opuntia basilaris*, one of the hardier species, has the evocative common name of 'beaver-tail prickly pear'; its fleshy pads (the tails of the beavers) are blue, red-purple or bronze in colour. More tender and still more desirable than this is the blue-blade, or dollar cactus, *O. macrocentra*, formerly, and descriptively, known as *O. violacea* because its large, flat, almost circular pads are the most extraordinary shade of blue tinged with violet-purple or mauve, or sometimes wholly mauve-purple.

In complete contrast to these agglomerations of circles and pads is the stark outline of the New Zealand lancewood tree, *Pseudopanax crassifolius*. In these pages we have met several plants with distinctive juvenile foliage; the lancewood goes through no less than four stages of development but it is the second that I want to extol. It quickly passes from the seedling stage to form a straight, unbranched stem set with long, narrow leaves, shaped like toothed rapiers and up to 90 cm (3 ft) long, and textured as though cut from metal. They point stiffly downwards at an angle of 45°, and for good measure they are dark bronze-green with a red midrib and maroon reverse. This stage lasts for about twenty years before, in adulthood, the lancewood develops a mixture of shorter sword-leaves and others composed of three to five leaflets.

CHAPTER 9

CULTIVATION

A PLANT'S PURPOSE in life is to perpetuate itself and most often it will do that by flowering and seeding. Leaves are merely part of the support system for keeping the plant alive so that it can fulfil its reproductive destiny. A plant that is stressed by unfavourable growing conditions will respond, more often than not, by putting all its energies into flowering and seeding to ensure at least that it may produce another generation, even if it does not itself survive. It will cut back on leaf production to concentrate on survival, making smaller and fewer leaves than normal. What does this mean in practical terms? Simply that, to get the best from your plants on your terms – lovely leaves – it helps to know what conditions to offer them.

TAKING TIPS FROM NATURE

Much of the beauty of leaves derives from the ways in which they have adapted to environmental conditions, above all, the climate and soil of their native region. The closer we match those conditions, the more likely plants are to thrive.

Plants with silver and grey foliage generally do best in full sun. Their felty or silky coating of tiny hairs is designed to reflect light so as to reduce the temperatures within the leaf tissue. In the wild they often grow where there are long spells without rain, so they need to conserve all the moisture they can; their felty coating also protects them against the desiccating effects of wind. In soggier climates they should be given sharply drained soil to compensate for the extra moisture at their roots. A waxy coating, such as that which gives the bluish cast to the Californian mahonias or to many eucalypts, also helps to reduce moisture loss. Even among hostas, which are at their best in cool, leafy soil, the varieties with glaucous foliage can withstand more sun than the green or variegated kinds.

Succulents are also designed to survive drought. Their fleshy leaves or stems have the capacity to store water. Therefore, they also need well-drained soil in wetter climates. The rosette structure of some succulents, such as agaves, is designed to capture every drop of moisture and direct it to the roots. This makes them vulnerable to rotting when excess water collects in the rosette base.

In contrast to the plants with thick and succulent leaves or a coating of wax or hairs are those with thin, often large, and hairless leaves. These are generally forest or woodland plants, adapted to making maximum use of low light levels and to shelter from drying winds. In the garden, they do best in shade, with shelter from wind and a cool, leafy soil about their roots. Large leaves of tough, leathery texture are likely to withstand more exposure than thin-textured ones.

Plants growing in sunny or windy places lose water from their leaves faster than those in sheltered or shady spots; so the drier your soil, the more scrupulously you should ensure that your moisture-lovers are spared the stress of a place fully in the sun or battered by winds. The plants will flower less freely in the shade but, when your first concern is beautiful foliage, that may not matter too much. Some plants that are thirsty for water, however, must be grown in full light to give of their best. *Rodgersia podophylla*, for example, is far more striking when its bold, web-footed leaves are bronzed by exposure to the light.

COLOURED OR VARIEGATED LEAVES

Plants with yellow-variegated leaves generally develop their best colour in sun, at least where the summers are not scorchingly hot and dry. Some – spotted laurels (*Aucuba japonica*) and the variegated elaeagnuses especially – keep their vivid colours in shade. Plants with all-gold leaves, especially if they are deciduous, need light shade to keep them from scorching; if given too much shade they will turn greenish. Depending on your climate and the microclimate of your garden, the answer may be shade during the hottest hours, or dappled shade all day.

Elaeagnus pungens 'Maculata' is as bright as you could wish, while Mahonia x media *'Charity' adds a strong, architectural note with its laddering leaves composed of holly-like leaflets.*

Purple foliage also turns to green – or rather, to a dirty shade of off-green – in shade. The solution here is to grow these plants in full sun, for the deepest, richest coppery purples. There are some exceptions: *Rosa glauca*, which is glaucous purple in sun and glaucous grey in shade; *Saxifraga fortunei* 'Wada'; *Euphorbia amygdaloïdes* 'Rubra'. The rhododendrons with mahogany purple in their foliage – 'Elizabeth Lockhart', 'Moser's Maroon' – also prefer part shade.

Plants with deciduous, white- or cream-variegated foliage need protection from the hottest sun, to save them from sunburn. Cream-variegated evergreens generally withstand more sun than white-variegated foliage, unless they are plants that even in their plain green form would do better in a shady place. Some variegated plants may flush with pink or purple if grown in full sun, though sometimes the trigger for the change of colour is the onset of cold weather. Sun brings out the best colour in plants selected for their many-toned variegations.

Plants with coloured spring foliage need careful placing; young growths are vulnerable to cold winds, untimely frosts or a sudden spell of hot sun. For the best autumn tints, on the other hand, an open place is best. Autumn-colouring trees and shrubs are seen at their most dramatic with the light behind them.

STARTING WITH THE SOIL

The starting point for success with plants, and above all with foliage plants, is the soil. Know the nature of your soil before you choose your plants; as with climate, you can do a certain amount to modify or improve it but its basic character will remain. Is it dry or moist, sandy, clay, chalk or – lucky you – a rich, deep loam? Does water drain away easily or lie stagnant? And above all, is it acid, neutral or alkaline? It is no good trying to grow lime-hating plants on alkaline soil. Nor is it any use trying to grow silvers and greys on moist, leafy soil in a high-rainfall area; they will spend more time looking dismally green than grey, even supposing they survive their first winter.

Hardly any plants grow well in poorly drained soil. If you find pools of water lying after rain, lay drains to take the water to a soakaway. If the problem is not too severe, you may be able to resolve it by the right choice of plants. I once cured a soggy patch in the middle of a sweep of heathers by planting the rosemary-leaved willow (*Salix elaeagnos*). It grew quickly and absorbed all the surplus water as it did so. Don't try to do both – lay drains and plant a shrub that is greedy for moisture; its roots will invade the drains and you will have to begin all over again.

If your soil is heavy and sticky, it can be improved by digging in generous quantities of garden compost or other humus-forming materials. You could also add some coarse grit at the same time, to help open the soil still more. Organic matter, plenty of it, is also the answer to a poor, light or stony soil; it helps to retain moisture and nourishes the plants at the same time. Shallow soils also benefit from generous applications of bulky organic materials. For most of us, the prime source of humus is the compost heap. Garden compost is environmentally sound, returning materials such as weeds, soft prunings, dead herbaceous topgrowths, and all your peelings and orange skins and tea leaves that would otherwise go into the dustbin and be wasted.

Willows not only look good beside water, but can also suck up excess moisture. This one, Salix alba *var.* sericea, *is a beautiful, silvery foliage plant as well.*

In the early days of a garden, building up a worthwhile quantity of compost may seem to take ages. Apart from the inevitable and expensive peat or ground bark, there may be leaves for the taking, or bracken nearby that you can cut, or perhaps a local farmer or stables will sell a load of manure cheaply. Other sources of humus are spent hops, spent mushroom compost, coco fibre.

Most of these are excellent as a mulch, to be applied each year to moist soil. Over the seasons the mulch will decompose and become incorporated into the soil, so ideally you should repeat the operation each year, in autumn before the frosts or in spring while the soil is still cool and moist. A mulch also helps to prevent the upper layers of soil drying out and moderates soil temperatures, keeping it cool in summer and warm in winter. Ground or chipped bark makes an expensive but aesthetic mulch; in the USA you may also find mulches of coco hulls or crushed peanut hulls.

Garden compost is fine as a mulch if your compost heap heats up enough to kill weed seeds; if it doesn't, it is safer to dig in compost than use it as a mulch. Partly rotted leaves make a first-rate mulch, especially for woodland plants. Gravel or chippings can also be used, particularly for plants that like free drainage and detest wet necks in winter; these, of course, add no humus to the soil.

The bulkier the organic material you add to your soil, the better. The chemical nutrients plants need can be applied in artificial form if need be. Remember that nitrogen is the element that makes for lush foliage but, if you do add artificial fertilizer, beware of giving variegated plants too much nitrogen or they may turn green. And, of course, keep your silvers and succulents on short commons; they are adapted to spartan living and will lose their character if overfed. Neither should a nitrogen-rich fertilizer be applied after midsummer because it will encourage soft growth that is vulnerable to frost. If a plant is looking miserable, a balanced foliar feed is often the best quick pick-me-up. With these provisos, there is no substitute for a high humus content in the soil. For fine foliage, even more than for abundant flowers or fruit, be generous with your soil and it will nourish and sustain your plants so that they can be generous with their leaves.

PLANTING

Provided that the soil is neither frozen nor waterlogged, you can plant container-grown plants, though if the soil is very dry you will need to take extra care and may prefer to keep the plant watered in its container until the drought has ended. Bare-rooted plants can be planted in autumn or spring, and hardy deciduous plants can be set in place during any open spell in the winter months. Evergreens are best planted in spring, when the soil is starting to warm up, except where the winters are not too severe, when they can be planted in early autumn. The more tender a plant, the less suitable it is for autumn planting.

Many garden centre plants will have had their growth hastened by protected cultivation and generous feeding and, if you buy them in autumn, they may be insufficiently hardened off to withstand frosts, even though the same plant with well-ripened growths may be perfectly hardy in your area. If in doubt, let the garden centre worry about overwintering, and buy – and plant – in spring.

The risk with spring planting is drought; not just dryness at the roots, but desiccating winds (and perhaps a late frost as well). It is always important to make sure that your new plantings are well watered-in; they may also need some temporary shelter from drying or chill winds. Container-grown plants should be soaked in a bucket of water before planting, to make sure the entire root ball is moist; bare-rooted plants should also be given a good drink and any damaged roots carefully pruned back with a clean cut. If the soil is dry, pour in a bucket or two of water before planting as well as watering-in afterwards.

If the soil is soggy and wet and you really cannot wait to plant until it dries somewhat, it is helpful to add to your planting mix of topsoil and garden compost a generous quantity of coarse grit. An open blend such as this will be easy to tease in among the roots. Be careful how you firm the soil lest you compact it into an airless block. At all other times, you will need to firm the plants in thoroughly to ensure the soil and the roots have made good contact as much as for safe anchorage.

It is important to give your trees and shrubs enough space to develop. Don't plant them too closely; if they once become distorted by jostling neighbours, they will never develop into shapely specimens. Some plants can be moved easily – most perennials and fibrous-rooted shrubs such as rhododendrons and griselinias, even when quite large. But many, including the most desirable, should be left alone once planted. Make sure your key plants, above all, have room to grow.

PRUNING

Once your shrubs start to grow, you will need to confront the question of pruning. Apart from the usual reasons for pruning – to keep the plants shapely

and healthy, remove damaged growths and encourage flowering or fruiting – some plants can be encouraged to produce foliage of exceptional size if they are cut hard back. The sumachs, *Rhus typhina* and *R. glabra*, make the most luxuriant fronds if cut back hard each year. Catalpas can be treated in the same way; a stooled golden catalpa, with its broad, chartreuse-yellow leaves, is a stunning sight. The silvery-grey willow, *Salix alba* var. *sericea*, one of the few greys to enjoy moist soils, also submits happily to annual stooling. All the elders (*Sambucus*) give of their best foliage if cut hard back and the purple hazel, *Corylus maxima* 'Purpurea', when stooled each year, is transformed from a good purple-leaved shrub to an outstanding one.

If you do not cut *Eucalyptus gunnii* and others with blue-glaucous juvenile foliage hard back each year, they will rush up into trees with much less exciting, willow-like, greenish leaves. Even *Rosa glauca* responds to hard pruning with much improved foliage, though this treatment will mean no flowers or fruit.

By cutting the variegated balsam poplar, *Populus* × *candicans* 'Aurora', hard back each spring you can not only keep it shrubby, but also ensure a supply of its pink

Below: *For foliage of tropical lushness,* Paulownia tomentosa *can be cut hard back each spring to produce a fresh supply of huge leaves.*

Opposite:*The best autumn colour belongs, more often than not, to hardy shrubs and trees. These can safely be planted from autumn to early spring, whenever the soil is neither waterlogged nor frozen.*

and white young foliage earlier in the season than on unpruned trees, which start green and later develop coloured leaves.

A tree or shrub that is pruned severely each year also goes on producing young growths for much longer than if left alone. The young leaves of many purple trees and shrubs have a ruby-like translucency lost by the older, coppery-purple or greenish-bronze foliage; hard pruning may mean four or five months of the appealing contrast between young and old, instead of a short burst in spring.

Some variegated plants are very apt to revert to plain green. The variegated box elders, *Acer negundo*, and elaeagnuses are notorious for it and, since the all-green shoots have much more vigour than the variegated, they can all too quickly take over if not removed as soon as spotted. If you leave them to grow to any size, they will leave a great gap in the shrub or tree's outline, which will probably never recover its balance. Prune the reverted shoots out at their point of origin, cutting as cleanly as you can; simply hacking them back will just spur them to greater activity. The variegated fuchsias, especially 'Versicolor', are also apt to produce green shoots; these can usually be yanked out at the base rather than cut.

KEEPING PESTS AND DISEASES AT BAY

Most garden pests and diseases, in one way or another, disfigure the plants they afflict. Hostas with their broad blades chewed to tatters by slugs, a variegated figwort, *Scrophularia auriculata* 'Variegata', with every ivory and jade leaf reduced to a skeleton by mullein shark caterpillars, or a variegated solomon's seal shredded by sawfly caterpillars, are hardly fulfilling their role as foliage plants. A pulmonaria afflicted with mildew is a travesty of its silvery or leopard-spotted self.

The best defence against both pests and diseases is good cultivation and scrupulous garden hygiene. Rare, however, is the garden that is free of slugs, aphids or fungal diseases of one kind or another. If you object to using chemical slug bait, you can try the old trick of putting out saucers of beer, or set grapefruit or melon rinds around the garden.

Always remove diseased foliage as soon as you see it and do not compost it. To keep mildew at bay, position susceptible plants where there is plenty of air movement. The trick with pulmonarias is to cut them to the ground the moment the leaves begin to look tired, after flowering, and give them a good drink, with liquid feed; new leaves will quickly develop and should stay fresh and clean all summer. If you find a particular plant looking diseased year after year, it is best to throw it out. There are so many fine foliage plants to choose from that there is no excuse for putting up with leaves that never look their best.

PLANTS WITH SILVER AND GREY FOLIAGE

Trees

Populus alba – D, 18 m (60 ft); silvery-white reverse

Pyrus salicifolia 'Pendula' – D, 4.5 m (15 ft); silver-grey

Salix alba var. *siricea* – D, 15 m (50 ft); grey-white

Tilia 'Petiolaris' – D, 18 m (60 ft); silver reverse

Shrubs

Artemisia arborescens – E, to 1.8 m (6 ft); silver

A. 'Powis Castle' – E, 90 cm (3 ft); silver

Atriplex halimus – D, 1.8 m (6 ft); silver-grey

Brachyglottis (syn. *Senecio*) *monroi* – E, 60 cm (2 ft); grey

B. (syn. *Senecio*) 'Sunshine' – E, 1.2 m (4 ft); grey-green

Buddleja alternifolia 'Argentea' – D, 3 m (10 ft); silvery

B. fallowiana – D, 1.8 m (6 ft); felted, grey-white

B. 'Lochinch' – D, 2.4 m (8 ft); felted, grey-white

Calluna vulgaris – E, 45 cm (18 in); grey-silver cvs include 'Silver Knight', 'Silver Queen'

Calocephalus brownii – E, 60 m (2 ft); silver

Cassinia vauvilliersii var. *albida* –

E, 1.2 m (4 ft); grey-white

Cistus albidus – E, 1.5 m (5 ft); woolly, grey-white

Convolvulus cneorum – E, 60 cm (2 ft); silvery white, silky

Cytisus battandieri – E, 4.5 m (15 ft); silver-grey

Elaeagnus angustifolia – D, 5.5 m (18 ft); grey-white

E. commutata – D, 1.5 m (5 ft); metallic silvery

Erica tetralix 'Alba Mollis' – E, 25 cm (10 in); grey-green

Euryops acraeus – E, 25 cm (10 in); platinum-white

Halimium atriplicifolium – E, 1.8 m (6 ft); grey-white

H. ocymoïdes – E, 60 cm (2 ft); grey-white

Helianthemum – E, 30 cm (12 in); several have grey foliage'

Helichrysum italicum – E, 60 cm (2 ft); silvery white

H. petiolare – E, 60 cm (2 ft); grey-felted

H. splendidum – E, 90 cm (3 ft); silver-felted

Hippophaë rhamnoïdes – D, 3 m (10 ft); grey

Lavandula dentata var. *candicans* – E, 60 cm (2 ft); grey-white

L. x *intermedia* Dutch group – E, 60 cm (2 ft); grey-white

L. lanata – E, 90 cm (3 ft); white-woolly

Leptospermum lanigerum 'Silver Sheen' – E, 1.8 m (6 ft); silvery

Lotus berthelotii – semi-E, trailing; silver, silky

Ozothamnus rosmarinifolius 'Silver Jubilee' – E, 1.2 m (4 ft); silvery grey

Phlomis italica – E, 75 cm (2½ ft); woolly, grey-white

Plecostachys serpyllifolia – E, spreading; silver-grey

Potentilla fruticosa 'Beesii' – D, 60 cm (2 ft); silver

P. fruticosa 'Manchu' – D, 30 cm (12 in); grey

P. fruticosa 'Vilmoriniana' – D, 1.2 m (4 ft); silvery grey

Rubus thibetanus – D, 1.2 m (4 ft); silvery grey

Salix elaeagnos – D, 1.8 m (6 ft); grey, white reverse

S. exigua – D, 3 m (10 ft); silvery white

S. helvetica – D, 60 cm (2 ft); grey

S. lanata – D, 90 cm (3 ft); grey-woolly

S. repens var. *argentea* – D, 60 cm (2 ft); white-felted

Santolina chamaecyparissus – E, 45 cm (18 in); white-woolly

S. pinnata ssp. *neapolitana* – E, 60 cm (2 ft); grey-white

CV = cultivar, D = deciduous, E = Evergreen

Senecio viravira (syn. *S. leucostachys*) – E, 60 cm (2 ft); silver

Teucrium fruticans – D, 1.5 m (5 ft); grey, white stems

Climbers

Vitis vinifera 'Incana' – D, 4.5 m (15 ft); grey

Perennials

Achillea 'Anthea' – E, 45 cm (18 in); silver

A. 'Moonshine' – D, 60 cm (2 ft); grey-green

Alyssum saxatile (syn. *Aurinia saxatilis*) – E, 25 cm (10 in); grey

Anaphalis margaritacea var. *cinnamomea* – D, 60 cm (2 ft); grey, white reverse

A. triplinervis – D, 35 cm (15 in); grey; whiter in 'Sommerschnee' ['Summer Snow']

Anthemis cupaniana – E, 30 cm (12 in); silver

Artemisia absinthium 'Lambrook Silver' – E, 90 cm (3 ft); pewter grey

A. splendens – D, 30 cm (12 in); silvery grey

A. ludoviciana – D, 1.2 m (4 ft); grey-white

A. ludoviciana var. *latiloba* – D, 60 cm (2 ft); grey-white

A. ludoviciana 'Silver Queen' – D, 60 cm (2 ft); grey-white

A. schmidtiana 'Nana' – D, 15 cm (6 in); silky, silver

A. stelleriana – D, 30 cm (12 in); grey-white, felted

Astelia nervosa var. *chathamica* 'Silver Spear' – E, 1.2 m (4 ft); silver

Ballota pseudodictamnus – D, 45 cm (18 in); woolly, grey

Celmisia coriacea – E, 30 cm (12 in); silver

Cerastium tomentosum var. *columnae* – E, 20 cm (8 in); silver-grey

Cynara cardunculus – D, 1.8 m (6 ft); silvery white

Dudleya farinosa – E, 15 cm (6 in); blue-white

Fascicularia spp. – E, 30 cm (12 in); grey-green

Gazania – E, 20 cm (8 in); cvs with silvery foliage include 'Cream Beauty', 'Silver Beauty'

Geranium traversii var. *elegans* – D, 15 cm (6 in); silver

Helichrysum 'Schweffellicht' ['Sulphur Light'] – D, 40 cm (16 in); grey

Heuchera 'Pewter Moon' – D, 30 cm (12 in); pewter grey, dark veins

Hieracium lanatum – D, 45 cm (18 in); white-felted

H. villosum – D, 30 cm (12 in); grey-woolly

Lamium galeobdolon – D, carpeter; cvs with silver-netted foliage include 'Silberteppich', 'Hermann's Pride'

L. maculatum – E, 15 cm (6 in); cvs with silver foliage include 'Beacon Silver', 'Red Nancy', 'Sterling Silver', 'White Nancy'

Lychnis coronaria – D, 75 cm (2½ ft); white-woolly

L. flos-jovis – D, 45 cm (18 in); grey-woolly

L. × *walkeri* 'Abbotswood Rose' – D, 75 cm (2½ ft); white-woolly

Potentilla atrosanguinea – D, 45 cm (18 in); silvery-silky

Pulmonaria saccharata Argentea group – E, 30 cm (12 in); heavily silver-splashed

P. vallarsae 'Margery Fish' – E, 30 cm (12 in); silver

Raoulia hookeri (*R. australis* of gardens) – E, prostrate; silver

Salvia argentea – E, 90 cm (3 ft); cobwebbed, grey-white

Scabiosa graminifolia – D, 45 cm (18 in); silver-grey

Sedum spathulifolium 'Cape Blanco' – E, 7 cm (3 in); white

Stachys byzantina – E, 60 cm (2 ft); woolly, white

Tanacetum densum-amani – E, 10 cm (4 in); silver

T. haradjanii – E, 10 cm (4 in); silver

Veronica spicata var. *incana* – E, 30 cm (12 in); silvery grey

Annuals, biennials and bedding plants

Centaurea cineraria ssp. *cineraria* (syn. *C. gymnocarpa*) – 30 cm (12 in); white

Onopordum acanthium – biennial, 2.1 m (7 ft); silver

Senecio cineraria – E, 60 cm (2 ft); silver-white

Verbascum bombyciferum – biennial, 2.4 m (8 ft); silver

V. olympicum – biennial, 1.8 m (6 ft); grey-felted

PLANTS WITH GLAUCOUS FOLIAGE

Trees

Acacia baileyana – E, 4.5 m
(15 ft); blue-grey

A. pravissima – E, 3 m (10 ft);
blue

Brahea armata – E, palm, 9 m
(30 ft); blue-grey

Eucalyptus coccifera – E, 12 m
(40 ft); grey-glaucous

E. globulus – E, 3 m (10 ft) if
hard-pruned; silvery blue

E. gunnii – E, 3 m (10 ft) if
hard-pruned; juvenile foliage
glaucous blue tinted mauve

E. perriniana – E, 4.5 m (15 ft);
silvery blue

Shrubs

Aethionema 'Warley Rose' – E,
15 cm (6 in); blue-grey

Berberis dictyophylla – D, 1.8 m
(6 ft); glaucous grey

B. temolaica – D, 3 m (10 ft);
glaucous blue

Coronilla valentina ssp. *glauca* –
E, 90 cm
(3 ft); glaucous blue

Cyathodes colensoi – E, 25 cm
(10 in); grey-mauve-
glaucous

Hebe albicans – E, 45 cm
(18 in); glaucous; 'Red
Edge' red-margined

H. carnosula – E, 45 cm (18 in);
glaucous grey

H. colensoi 'Glauca' – E, 60 cm
(2 ft); glaucous

H. cupressoïdes – E, 75 cm (2½
ft); blue-grey

H. 'Pewter Dome' – E, 60 cm
(2 ft); glaucous grey

H. pimeleoïdes 'Quicksilver' –
E, 30 cm (12 in); blue-grey

H. pinguifolia 'Pagei' – E,
25 cm (10 in); grey-glaucous

Opuntia basilaris – E, spreading;
blue, sometimes red or
bronze

O. macrocentra – E, 1.5 m (5 ft);
blue-grey flushed mauve

Rhododendron cinnabarinum
Concatenans group – E,
1.5 m (5 ft); glaucous blue

R. impeditum 'Blue Steel' – E,
30 cm (12 in); steel blue

R. lepidostylum – E, 45 cm
(18 in); glaucous blue

Rosa glauca – D, 2.4 m (8 ft);
glaucous grey in shade

Ruta graveolens 'Jackman's Blue'
– E, 60 cm (2 ft); blue-
glaucous

Climbers

Lonicera splendida – D, 4 m
(13 ft); glaucous blue

Rosa 'Wickwar' – D, 6 m
(20 ft); blue grey

Conifers

Abies concolor 'Compacta' – E,
75 cm (2½ ft); grey-blue

Chamaecyparis lawsoniana 'Bleu
Nantais' – E, 1.2 m (4 ft);
blue

C. lawsoniana 'Chilworth
Silver' – E, 3 m (10 ft);
silvery blue

C. lawsoniana 'Pembury Blue' –
E, 9 m (30 ft); pale grey-blue

C. lawsoniana 'Silver Queen' –
E, 3 m (10 ft); silver-green

C. lawsoniana 'Triomf van
Boskoop' – E, 18 m (60 ft);
blue-grey

C. lawsoniana 'White Spot' – E,
1.8 m (6 ft); silvery green

C. pisifera 'Boulevard' – E,
1.2 m (4 ft); bright blue-grey

Cupressus arizonica 'Blue Ice' –
E, 1.5 m (5 ft); blue-grey

Cupressus torulosa 'Cashmeriana'
– E, 6 m (20 ft); grey-blue

Juniperus horizontalis – E,
prostrate; glaucous cvs
include 'Bar Harbor', 'Blue
Chip', 'Hughes', 'Wiltonii'

J. scopulorum 'Blue Heaven' –
E, 2.4 m (8 ft); silvery blue

J. scopulorum 'Moonglow' – E,
2.4 m (8 ft); blue-grey

J. scopulorum 'Skyrocket' – E,
3 m (10 ft); steely blue

J. squamata 'Blue Carpet' – E,
prostrate; silvery blue

J. squamata 'Blue Star' – E,
semi-prostrate; blue-grey

J. squamata 'Meyeri' – E, 3 m
(10 ft); dark blue-glaucous

J. virginiana 'Grey Owl' – E,
spreading; grey-blue

Picea pungens – E, to 2.4 m
(8 ft); blue-glaucous cvs
include 'Globosa' (dwarf),
'Hoopsii', 'Hoto', 'Koster',
'Moerheimii'

Pinus ayacahuite – E, 9 m
(30 ft); blue-grey

Perennials

Acaena 'Blue Haze' – E,
carpeting; pewter blue

Agave franzosinii – E, 2.4 m (8
ft); glaucous white

Aquilegia flabellata – D, 30 cm
(12 in); glaucous grey

Argyranthemum foeniculaceum
'Royal Haze' – E, 90 cm
(3 ft); blue-grey

A. maderense – E, 45 cm
(18 in); blue-grey

Athyrium niponicum var. *pictum*
– D, 30 cm (12 in); glaucous
grey

Beschorneria yuccoïdes – E, 1.8 m
(6 ft); blue-grey

Crambe maritima – D, 60 cm
(2 ft); glaucous white

Dianthus – E, mat-forming;
glaucous

Dicentra formosa 'Stuart
Boothman' – D, 30 cm
(12 in); steel-blue

D. 'Langtrees' – D, 30 cm
(12 in); glaucous grey

Echeveria – E, to 20 cm (8 in);
several grey, blue or lilac

Eryngium maritimum – D, 30 cm

(12 in); glaucous grey

Erysimum 'Bowles' Mauve' – E,
75 cm (2½ ft); steely grey

Euphorbia myrsinites – E, 15 cm
(6 in); glaucous grey

E. nicaeënsis – D, 60 cm (2 ft);
glaucous grey-blue

E. rigida – E, 45 cm (18 in);
glaucous grey

E. seguierana ssp. *niciciana* – D,
45 cm (18 in); glaucous

Hosta 'Big Daddy' – D, 75 cm
(2½ ft); very blue

H. 'Krossa Regal' D, 90 cm (3
ft); glaucous, white reverse

H. sieboldiana var. *elegans* – D,
75 cm (2½ ft); glaucous blue

H. tokudama – D, 45 cm
(18 in); glaucous blue

H. × *tardiana* – D, 30 cm
(12 in); very blue-glaucous
cvs include 'Blue Moon',
'Blue Wedgwood',
'Buckshaw Blue', 'Hadspen
Blue', 'Halcyon'

Iris pallida var. *dalmatica* – D,
1.2 m (4 ft); blue-grey

Kniphofia caulescens – E, 1.2 m
(4 ft); blue-grey

Lysimachia ephemerum – D,
90 cm (3 ft); glaucous grey

Macleaya – D, 1.8 m (6 ft); all
grey-green above, white
reverse

Melianthus major – D, 2.4 m
(8 ft); grey-glaucous

Mertensia ciliata – D, 60 cm
(2 ft); blue-grey glaucous

Othonna cheirifolia – E, 20 cm
(8 in); glaucous

Parahebe perfoliata – D, 60 cm
(2 ft); blue-grey

Rudbeckia maxima – 1.2 m
(4 ft); glaucous blue

Sedum anacampseros – E, 10 cm

(4 in); blue-grey

S. cauticola – D, 15 cm (6 in);
glaucous blue-grey

S. 'Herbstfreude' ['Autumn
Joy'] – D, 75 cm (2½ ft);
glaucous

S. sieboldii – D, 20 cm (8 in);
glaucous

S. spectabile – D, 45 cm (18 in);
glaucous green

S. 'Sunset Cloud' – D, 30 cm
(12 in); darkly glaucous

Sisyrinchium striatum – E, 60 cm
(2 ft); glaucous

Thalictrum flavum var. *glaucum*
(syn. *T. f.* var. *speciosissimum*)
– 1.8 m (6 ft); glaucous

Yucca whipplei – E, 90 cm (3 ft);
blue

Grasses

Elymus glaucus – D, 1.2 m
(4 ft); glaucous blue

E. magellanicus – D, 45 cm
(18 in); silvery blue

Festuca amethystina – D, 20 cm
(8 in); lilac-glaucous

F. glauca – D, 20 cm (8 in);
blue-grey. 'Blaufuchs' ['Blue
Fox'] brightest

F. valesiaca 'Silbersee' ['Silver
Sea'] – D, 15 cm (6 in);
blue-glaucous

Helictotrichon sempervirens –
1.2 m (4 ft); glaucous blue

Leymus arenarius – D, 1.2 m
(4 ft); blue-grey

Annuals and biennials

Glaucium flavum and *G.
corniculatum* – biennial,
60 cm (2 ft); blue-grey

Omphalodes linifolia – annual,
25 cm (10 in); grey-glaucous

PLANTS WITH GOLDEN FOLIAGE

Trees

Acer cappadocicum 'Aureum' – D, 12 m (40 ft); rich yellow

A. negundo 'Auratum' – D, 9 m (30 ft); yellow

A. pseudoplatanus 'Worleei' – D, 12 m (40 ft); yellow

Alnus incana 'Aurea' – D, 6 m (20 ft); yellow

Betula pendula 'Golden Cloud' – D, 6 m (20 ft); yellow

Catalpa bignonioïdes 'Aurea' – D, 6 m (20 ft); yellow

Fagus sylvatica 'Zlatia' – D, very slow; yellow

F. sylvatica 'Dawyck Gold' – D, 12 m (40 ft); yellow

Gleditsia triacanthos 'Sunburst' – D, 9 m (30 ft); lime yellow

Populus alba 'Richardii' – D, 6 m (20 ft); golden, white reverse

Quercus robur 'Concordia' – D, 4.5 m (15 ft); yellow

Robinia pseudoacacia 'Frisia' – D, 15 m (50 ft); bright yellow

Sorbus aria 'Chrysophylla' – D, 15 m (50 ft); yellow

S. aucuparia 'Dirkenii' – D, 9 m (30 ft); yellow

Shrubs

Acer shirasawanum (syn. *A. japonicum*) *aureum* – D, 4 m (13 ft); yellow

Berberis thunbergii 'Aurea' – D, 90 cm (3 ft); lime-yellow

Calluna vulgaris – E, 20 cm (8 in); gold cvs include 'Beoley Gold', 'Gold Haze', 'Golden Feather' (soft orange in winter), 'Golden Carpet', 'Joy Vanstone', 'Serlei Aurea'

Caryopteris x *clandonensis* 'Worcester Gold' – D, 45 cm (18 in); lime

Cassinia fulvida – E, 90 cm (3 ft); golden

Choisya ternata 'Sundance' – E, 1.2 m (4 ft); bright yellow

Cornus alba 'Aurea' – D, 1.8 m (6 ft); lime-yellow

C. mas 'Aurea' – D, 2.4 m (8 ft); soft yellow

Corylus avellana 'Aurea' – D, 1.8 m (6 ft); lime-yellow

Erica arborea 'Albert's Gold' – E, 1.5 m (5 ft); yellow

E. carnea – E, 30 cm (12 in); yellow to chartreuse cvs include 'Aurea', 'Foxhollow'

E. cinerea – E, 30 cm (12 in); yellow to copper cvs include 'Golden Hue' (red in winter)

E. × *darleyensis* 'Jack H. Brummage' – E, 45 cm (18 in); yellow

E. erigena 'Golden Lady' – E, 60 cm (2 ft); bright yellow

E. vagans 'Valerie Proudley' – E, 20 cm (8 in); bright yellow

Escallonia 'Gold Brian' – E, 75 cm (2½ ft); bright gold

Euonymus fortunei 'Sheridan Gold' – E, 60 cm (2 ft); golden to green

Fuchsia 'Genii' – D, 1.2 m (4 ft); lime yellow

F. magellanica 'Aurea' – D, 1.2 m (4 ft); lime yellow

Hebe ochracea 'James Stirling' – E, 25 cm (10 in); old gold

Helichrysum petiolare 'Limelight' – E, 60 cm (2 ft); lime

Hypericum x *inodorum* 'Summergold' – D, 90 cm (3 ft); yellow

Lonicera nitida 'Baggesen's Gold' – E, 1.2 m (4 ft); cream to yellow

Philadelphus coronarius 'Aureus' – D, 1.8 m (6 ft); yellow

Physocarpus opulifolius 'Luteus' and 'Dart's Gold' – D, 1.8 m (6 ft); bright yellow

Pittosporum tenuifolium – E, 3 m (10 ft); yellow cvs include 'Golden King', 'Warnham Gold', 'Winter Sunshine'

Ptelea trifoliata 'Aurea' – D, 4.5 m (15 ft); soft yellow

Ribes sanguineum 'Brocklebankii' – D, 1.2 m (4 ft); yellow

Rubus cockburnianus 'Golden Vale' – D, 1 m (3½ ft); lime yellow

R. idaeus 'Aureus' – D, 90 cm (3 ft); bright yellow

R. parviflorus 'Sunshine Spreader' – D, spreading; yellow

Sambucus nigra 'Aurea' – D, 2.4 m (8 ft); yellow-green

S. racemosa 'Plumosa Aurea' and 'Sutherland Gold' – D, 2.4 m (8 ft); bronze-yellow

Spiraea japonica 'Golden Princess' – D, 60 cm (2 ft); bright gold

Weigela 'Looymansii Aurea' – D, 2.1 m (7 ft); yellow

Climbers

Hedera helix 'Angularis Aurea' – E, 2.4 m (8 ft); suffused yellow

H. helix 'Buttercup' – E, 1.2 m (4 ft); yellow

Humulus lupulus 'Aureus' – herbaceous, 2.4 m (8 ft); lime yellow

Conifers

Abies koreana 'Flava' ('Aurea') – E, 1.2 m (4 ft); yellow

A. nordmanniana 'Golden Spreader' – E, prostrate, bright yellow

Cedrus deodara 'Aurea' – E, 4.5 m (15 ft); yellow to lime

C. deodara 'Nana Aurea' – E, 3 m (10 ft); yellow

C. deodara 'Golden Horizon' – E, 60 cm (2 ft); yellow

Chamaecyparis lawsoniana 'Lane' – E, 9 m (30 ft); golden yellow

C. lawsoniana 'Minima Aurea' – E, 60 cm (2 ft); yellow

C. lawsoniana 'Moonshine' – E, 2.1 m (7 ft); golden yellow

C. lawsoniana 'Stewartii' – E, 12 m (40 ft); yellow

C. obtusa 'Crippsii' – E, 4.5 m (15 ft); yellow

C. obtusa 'Nana Lutea' – E, 60 cm (2 ft); yellow

C. pisifera 'Filifera Aurea' – E, 1.2 m (4 ft); golden

C. pisifera 'Gold Spangle' – E, 75 cm (2½ ft); yellow

Cryptomeria japonica 'Sekkan Sugi' – E, 3 m (10 ft); yellow to cream

Cupressus macrocarpa – E, 9 m (30 ft); yellow cvs include 'Donard Gold', 'Goldcrest'

C. sempervirens 'Swane's Gold' – E, 3 m (10 ft); yellow

Juniperus chinensis 'Aurea' – E, 3 m (10 ft); yellow

J. communis 'Gold Cone' – E, 1.2 m (4 ft); yellow

J. × media 'Gold Coast' – E, 45 cm (18 in); bright gold

J. × media 'Old Gold' – E, 90 cm (3 ft); bronzed gold

J. × media 'Sulphur Spray' – E, 90 cm (3 ft); sulphur yellow

Taxus baccata 'Semperaurea' – E, 1.5 m (5 ft); old-gold

T. baccata 'Standishii' – E, 1.5 m (5 ft); yellow

T. baccata 'Summergold' – E, semi-prostrate; gold

Thuja occidentalis 'Rheingold' – E, 1.2 m (4 ft); old gold to copper

T. orientalis 'Aurea Nana' – E, 75 cm (2½ ft); golden green

T. plicata 'Stoneham Gold' – E, 90 cm (3 ft); yellow-bronze

Perennials

Campanula garganica 'Dickson's Gold' – D, 15 cm (6 in); yellow

Centaurea montana 'Gold Bullion' – D, 30 cm (12 in); chartreuse yellow

Chrysanthemum parthenium 'Aureum' – D, 45 cm (18 in); bright yellow

Filipendula ulmaria 'Aurea' – D, 60 cm (2 ft); lime yellow

Hosta fortunei var *albopicta* f. *aurea* – D, 60 cm (2 ft); yellow then lime green

H. 'Golden Prayers' – D, 30 cm (12 in); yellow

H. 'Hydon Sunset' – D, 45 cm (18 in); yellow

H. 'Piedmont Gold' – D, 45 cm (18 in); yellow

H. 'Sum and Substance' – D, 60 cm (2 ft); lime yellow

H. 'Wogon' – D, 30 cm (12 in); yellow

H. 'Zounds' – D, 60 cm (2 ft); yellow

Lysimachia nummularia 'Aurea' – E, carpeter; lime yellow

Origanum vulgare 'Aureum' – D, 10 cm (4 in); golden green

Sedum acre 'Aureum' – D, 2 cm (under 1in); yellow-tipped

Soleirolia (syn. *Helxine*) *soleirolii* 'Aurea' – E, 1 cm (½ in); yellow

Thymus x *citriodorus* 'Aureus' – E, 10 cm (4 in); yellow

T. x *citriodorus* 'Bertram Anderson' – E, 3 cm (1in); bright yellow

Grasses

Alopecurus pratensis 'Aureus' – D, 20 cm (8 in); yellow

Deschampsia flexuosa 'Tatra Gold' – D, 60 cm (2 ft); lime yellow

Milium effusum 'Aureum' – D, 60 cm (2 ft); golden yellow

PLANTS WITH YELLOW-VARIEGATED FOLIAGE

Trees

Acer negundo 'Elegans' – D, 9 m
(30 ft); yellow-margined

Castanea sativa 'Variegata' – D,
7 m (23 ft); yellow-margined

Cornus florida 'Rainbow' – D,
4.5 m (15 ft); yellow-edged

Ligustrum lucidum 'Excelsum
Superbum' – E, 6 m (20 ft);
yellow- and cream-splashed

Liriodendron tulipiferum
'Aureomarginatum' – D,
15 m (50 ft); yellow-
margined

Shrubs

Abutilon megapotamicum
'Variegatum' – D, 1.8 m
(6 ft); yellow-mottled

A. × *milleri* 'Variegatum' – D,
1.8 m (6 ft); yellow-mottled

Aralia elata 'Aureovariegata' –
D, 2.4 m (8 ft); yellow-
variegated fading to cream

Aucuba japonica – E, 2.4 m (8
ft); yellow-variegated cvs
include 'Crotonifolia', 'Gold
Dust', 'Variegata' (yellow-
flecked), 'Picturata' (yellow-
splashed in centre),
'Sulphurea Marginata'

Coprosma 'Beatson's Gold' – E,
1.8 m (6 ft); dark green and
gold

Cornus alba 'Spaethii' – D,
1.8 m (6 ft); yellow-edged

Elaeagnus × *ebbingei* 'Gilt Edge'
– E, 2.4 m (8 ft); yellow-
margined

E. × *ebbingei* 'Limelight' – E,
2.4 m (8 ft); yellow-centred

E. pungens 'Maculata' – E,
2.4 m (8 ft); yellow-centred

Euonymus fortunei – E, 60 cm
(2 ft); yellow-variegated cvs
include 'Emerald 'n' Gold',
'Sunspot'

E. japonicus – E, 2.4 m (8 ft);
yellow-variegated cvs
include 'Aureus', 'Ovatus
Aureus'

Hydrangea macrophylla 'Tricolor'
– D, 1.2 m (4 ft); cream,
yellow and grey-green

Ilex x *altaclarensis* – E, 6 m
(20 ft); yellow-variegated cvs
include 'Golden King',
'Lawsoniana'

I. aquifolium – E, 6 m (20 ft);
yellow-variegated cvs
include 'Golden Milkboy',
'Golden Queen', 'Golden
Van Tol', 'Madame Briot',
'Myrtifolia Aureo Maculata'

Ligustrum ovalifolium 'Aureum'
– E, 2.4 m (8 ft); yellow-
margined

Luma apiculata (syn. *Myrtus
apiculatus*) 'Glanleam Gold' –

E, 1.5 m (5 ft); broadly
yellow-margined

Metrosideros kermadecensis – E,
1.8 m (6 ft); 'Radiant'
yellow, green-edged;
'Variegatus' yellow-
margined

Osmanthus heterophyllus
'Aureomarginatus' – E,
1.8 m (6 ft); yellow-edged

Pittosporum tenuifolium
'Abbotsbury Gold' – E,
2.4 m (8 ft); yellow-splashed

Pseudopanax lessonii 'Gold
Splash' – E, 1.8 m (6 ft);
yellow-blotched

Salvia officinalis 'Icterina' – E,
45 cm (18 in); lime-edged

Sambucus nigra
'Aureomarginata' – D, 3 m
(10 ft); yellow-edged

Vinca minor 'Aureovariegata' –
E, 30 cm (12 in); yellow-
splashed

Weigela 'Florida Variegata' – D,
1.8 m (6 ft); yellow-edged

Climbers

Hedera colchica 'Dentata
Variegata' – E, 4 m (13 ft);
yellow-margined

H. colchica 'Sulphur Heart' – E,
4 m (13 ft); yellow-splashed

H. helix 'Goldheart' – E, 3 m
(10 ft); yellow-centred

Jasminum officinale 'Aureum' –
D, 4 m (13 ft); heavily
yellow-splashed

Conifers

Juniperus x *media* 'Blue and
Gold' – E, 1.2 m (4 ft);
blue-grey and cream
Taxus baccata 'Repens Aurea' –
E, 60 cm (2 ft); yellow-
margined
Thuja plicata 'Zebrina' – E,
18 m (60 ft); yellow-
speckled

Perennials

Acorus gramineus 'Ogon' – E,
20 cm (8 in); bright gold-
variegated
Agave americana – E, 1.8 m
(6 ft); yellow-variegated in
'Marginata' and 'Variegata'
Aptenia cordifolia 'Variegata' –
E, 5 cm (2 in); creamy
yellow, brighter edged
Aquilegia vulgaris 'Woodside' –
D, 60 cm (2 ft); creamy
yellow on blue
Arabis ferdinandi-coburgii 'Old
Gold' – E, 5 cm (2 in);
yellow-edged
Aubrieta 'Aureovariegata' – D,
7 cm (3 in); yellow-
margined
Brunnera macrophylla 'Hadspen
Cream' – D, 45 cm (18 in);
creamy-yellow-margined
Canna malawiensis 'Variegata' –
D, 1.2 m (4 ft); yellow-
striped
Convallaria majalis 'Vic
Pawlowski's Gold' – D,
20 cm (8 in); gold-striped
Hosta fortunei var. *albopicta* – D,
60 cm (2 ft); yellow-centred

H. fortunei var. *aureomarginata*
('Obscura Marginata') – D,
60 cm (2 ft); yellow-edged
H. 'Gold Standard' – D, 45 cm
(18 in); yellow
H. 'Shade Fanfare' – D, 45 cm
(18 in); creamy
H. sieboldiana 'Frances
Williams' – D, 60 cm (2 ft);
grey-blue, yellow-margined
H. tokudama f. *aureonebulosa* –
D, 45 cm (18 in); blue-grey,
yellow-suffused and striped
H. tokudama f. *flavocircinalis* –
D, 45 cm (18 in); blue-grey,
yellow-edged
H. ventricosa var. *aureomaculata* –
D, 90 cm (3 ft); mid-yellow-
splashed
H. ventricosa 'Aureomarginata'
– D, 90 cm (3 ft); yellow-
edged
H. 'Wide Brim' – D, 35 cm
(15 in); yellow-margined
Iris pallida 'Variegata' – D,
90 cm (3 ft); grey, yellow-
striped
Liriope muscari 'Gold Banded' –
E, 30 cm (12 in); yellow-
striped
Osteospermum 'Bodegas Pink' –
D, 45 cm (18 in); creamy-
yellow-variegated
Phormium cookianum 'Cream
Delight' – E, 90 cm (3 ft);
cream-striped
P. 'Yellow Wave' – E, 1.2 m
(4 ft); yellow-striped
Sedum alboroseum
'Mediovariegatum' – D,
30 cm (12 in); grey-green,
creamy-yellow-centred
Thymus x *citriodorus* 'Golden
King' – E, 20 cm (10 in);
gold-edged

T. 'Doone Valley' – E, 10 cm
(4 in); yellow-splashed
Tolmeia menziesii 'Taff's Gold'
– E, 20 cm (8 in); yellow-
freckled on pale green
Yucca filamentosa – E, 45 cm
(18 in); yellow-variegated
cvs include 'Bright Edge',
'Variegata'
Y. flaccida 'Golden Sword' – E,
60 cm (2 ft); yellow-striped
Y. gloriosa 'Variegata' – E,
1.2 m (4 ft); yellow-striped

Grasses, sedges and bamboos

Alopecurus pratensis
'Aureovariegatus' – D,
20 cm (8 in); yellow-striped
Carex elata 'Aurea' – D, 60 cm
(2 ft); bright yellow-striped
C. hachijoensis 'Evergold' – E,
30 cm (12 in); yellow-
striped
C. morrowii 'Fisher's Form'- E,
40 cm (16 in); yellow-
margined
Cortaderia selloana 'Gold Band'
– D, 1.2 m (4 ft); yellow-
striped
Hakonechloa macra 'Alboaurea' –
D, 30 cm (12 in); bright
yellow-striped
H. macra 'Aureola' – D, 30 cm
(12 in); bright yellow-striped
Miscanthus sinensis 'Zebrinus' –
1.5 m (5 ft); horizontally
yellow-banded
Pleioblastus auricomus
(syn. *Arundinaria viridistriata*)
– E, 1.5 m (5 ft) bamboo;
bright yellow-striped
Spartina pectinata
'Aureomarginata' – D, 1.2 m
(4 ft); yellow-striped

PLANTS WITH WHITE– OR CREAM-VARIEGATED FOLIAGE

Trees

Acer negundo 'Variegatum' – D, 9 m (30 ft); white-margined

A. platanoïdes 'Drummondii' – D, 15 m (50 ft); white-edged

Castanea sativa 'Albomarginata' – D, 18 m (60 ft); white-margined

Ligustrum lucidum 'Tricolor' – E, 6 m (20 ft); white-edged

Shrubs

Acer palmatum 'Butterfly' – D, 3 m (10 ft); white-margined

Aralia elata 'Variegata' – D, 2.4 m (8 ft); white-edged

Azara microphylla 'Variegata' – E, 2.4 m (8 ft); cream-variegated

Buddleja davidii 'Harlequin' – D, 2.4 m (8 ft); cream-edged

Buxus sempervirens 'Elegantissima' – E, 1.2 m (4 ft); cream-edged

Cordyline australis 'Torbay Dazzler' – E, to 3 m (10 ft); cream

Cornus alba 'Elegantissima' – D, 2.4 m (8 ft); white-margined

C. alternifolia 'Argentea' – D, 2.4 m (8 ft); white-edged

C. controversa 'Variegata' – D, 5 m (18 ft); bold cream-variegated

C. mas 'Variegata' – D, 2.4 m (8 ft); white-edged

Coronilla valentina 'Variegata' – E, 90 cm (3 ft); grey and cream

Cotoneaster horizontalis 'Variegata' – D, 60 cm (2 ft); white-edged

Euonymus fortunei 'Emerald Gaiety' – E, 60 cm (2 ft); white-margined

E. fortunei 'Silver Queen' – E, 1.2 m (4 ft); creamy white-variegated

E. fortunei 'Variegatus' – E, 60 cm (2 ft); white-edged

Euonymus japonicus 'Latifolius Albomarginatus' – E, 1.2 m (4 ft); white-margined

E. japonicus 'Microphyllus Albovariegatus' – E, 90 cm (3 ft); white-edged

Fatsia japonica 'Variegata' – E, 3 m (10 ft); cream-margined

Fuchsia magellanica var. *gracilis* 'Variegata' – D, 60 cm (2 ft); ivory-white-margined

F. magellanica var. *molinae* 'Sharpitor' – D, 1.2 m (4 ft); cream-edged

Griselinia littoralis – E, 3 m (10 ft); 'Bantry Bay' and 'Dixon's Cream' with cream splash in centre, 'Variegata' ivory-margined

Hebe × *andersonii* 'Variegata' – E, 1.2 m (4 ft); ivory and grey

H. 'Carnea Variegata' – E, 90 cm (3 ft); cream-splashed, pink in winter

H. × *franciscana* 'Variegata' – E, 60 cm (2 ft); broadly cream-margined

Ilex aquifolium – E, 6 m (20 ft); white- or cream-variegated cvs include 'Argentea Marginata', 'Argentea Marginata Pendula', 'Ferox Argentea', 'Handsworth New Silver', 'Silver Milkmaid', 'Silver Queen'

Kerria japonica 'Picta' – D, 1.2 m (4 ft); grey-green, cream-edged

Osmanthus heterophyllus 'Variegatus' – E, 1.5 m (5 ft); cream-margined

Philadelphus coronarius 'Variegatus' – D, 1.8 m (6 ft); white-margined

Pieris japonica 'Variegata' – E, 1.2 m (4 ft); white-edged

Pittosporum eugenioïdes 'Variegatum' – E, 3 m (10 ft); pale green, cream-margined

P. tenuifolium 'Irene Patterson' – E, 1.8 m (6 ft); heavily white-spotted

P. tenuifolium 'Silver Queen' –
E, 3 m (10 ft); white-
margined

P. tobira 'Variegatum' – E, 3 m
(10 ft); white-margined

Potentilla fruticosa 'Abbotswood
Silver' – D, 60 cm (2 ft);
white-edged

Prunus laurocerasus
'Castlewellan' (syn. 'Marbled
White') – E, 1.5 m (5 ft);
heavily ivory-white-mottled

P. lusitanica 'Variegata' – E,
2.1 m (7 ft); white-edged

Pyracantha 'Sparkler' – E, 1.2 m
(4 ft); white-edged

Rhamnus alaternus
'Argenteovariegata' – E, 3 m
(10 ft); grey, white-edged

Rhododendron ponticum
'Variegatum' – E, 1.8 m
(6 ft); cream-margined

Rubus microphyllus 'Variegatus'
– D, 60 cm (2 ft); white-
edged

Sambucus nigra 'Pulverulenta' –
D, 1.8 m (6 ft); heavily
white-splashed

Viburnum tinus 'Variegatum' –
E, 1.8 m (6 ft); ivory-cream-
variegated

Vinca major 'Variegata' – E,
60 cm (2 ft); cream-edged

V. minor 'Argenteovariegata' –
E, 30 cm (12 in); white-
edged

Weigela 'Praecox Variegata' – D,
1.5 m (5 ft); white-margined

Climbers

Hedera algeriensis 'Gloire de
Marengo' – E, 4 m (13 ft);
white- and grey-marbled

H. helix – E; white-variegated
cvs include 'Adam', 'Glacier',

'Luzii', 'Sagittifolia Variegata'

Jasminum officinale
'Argenteovariegatum' – D,
4.5 m (15 ft); white-
variegated

Conifers

Chamaecyparis lawsoniana
'Albospica' – E, 4.5 m
(15 ft); white-tipped

C. lawsoniana 'Albovariegata' –
E, 75 cm (2½ ft); white-
patched

C. lawsoniana 'Pygmaea
Argentea' – E, 45 cm
(18 in); white-tipped

C. lawsoniana 'Silver Threads' –
E, 1.2 m (4 ft); lime green
and cream

C. lawsoniana 'Snow White' –
E, 1.2 m (4 ft); blue-green,
white-tipped

C. lawsoniana 'White Spot' – E,
1.8 m (6 ft); silvery green,
white-tipped

Sequoia sempervirens 'Adpressa' –
E, 90 cm (3 ft); cream-tipped

Perennials

Acorus calamus 'Variegatus' – D,
90 cm (3 ft); cream-striped

Aegopodium podagraria
'Variegata' – D, 20 cm
(8 in); cream-splashed

Agave americana 'Mediopicta' –
E, 1.2 m (4 ft); white-
variegated in centre

Ajuga reptans 'Variegata' – E,
10 cm (4 in); grey and ivory

Alyssum saxatile 'Dudley
Neville Variegated' – D,
10 cm (4 in); cream

Arabis caucasica 'Variegata' – E,
15 cm (6 in); cream-edged

A. ferdinandi-coburgii 'Variegata'

– E, 5 cm (2 in); white-
variegated

Arum italicum var. *pictum* – D,
winter-green, 45 cm (18 in);
white-marbled

Aubrieta 'Argenteovariegata' –
D, 7 cm (3 in); white-
variegated

Brunnera macrophylla 'Dawson's
White' – D, 45 cm (18 in);
white-margined

Erysimum linifolium
'Variegatum' – E, 45 cm
(18 in); grey, ivory-margined

Felicia amelloïdes 'Variegata' – E,
15 cm (6 in); cream

Geranium phaeum 'Variegatum'
– D, 45 cm (18 in); white-
variegated

Hemerocallis fulva 'Kwanzo
Variegata' – D, 90 cm (3 ft);
white-striped

Heuchera 'Snow Storm' – E,
30 cm (12 in); heavily
white-flecked

H. 'Taff's Joy' – E, 30 cm
(12 in); white-flecked

Hosta crispula – D, 75 cm (2½
ft); white margined

H. fortunei 'Albomarginata' –
D, 75 cm (2½ ft); white-
margined

H. 'Francee' – D, 60 cm (2 ft);
white-edged

H. 'Ground Master' – D,
30 cm (12 in); ivory-edged

H. rohdeifolia (syn. *H.
helonioïdes*) f. albopicta – D,
30 cm (12 in); cream-edged

H. sieboldii – D, 50 cm (20 in);
cream-margined

H. undulata 'Albomarginata'
(syn. *H.* 'Thomas Hogg') –
D, 45 cm (18 in); white-
margined

H. undulata var. *undulata* – D, 45 cm (18 in); white-splashed

H. undulata var. *univittata* – D, 45 cm (18 in); white-splashed

Iris foetidissima 'Variegata' – E, 60 cm (2 ft); white-striped

I. japonica 'Variegata' – D, 30 cm (12 in); white-striped

I. laevigata 'Variegata' – D, 45 cm (18 in); white-striped

I. pallida 'Argentca Variegata' – D, 75 cm (2½ ft); grey, white-striped

I. tectorum 'Variegata' – E, 30 cm (12 in); cream-striped

Liriope muscari 'John Burch' – E, 30 cm (12 in); cream-striped

L. 'Silvery Sunproof' – E, 30 cm (12 in); heavily white-striped

Mentha suaveolens (syn. *M. rotundifolia*) 'Variegata' – D, 30 cm (12 in); white-splashed

Ophiopogon jaburan 'Vittatus' ('Variegatus') – E, 30 cm (12 in); white-striped

Osteospermum 'Silver Sparkler' – D, 30 cm (12 in); white-variegated

Persicaria (syn. *Tovara*) *virginiana* 'Variegata' – D, 60 cm (2 ft); cream-striped

Phlox paniculata – D, 90 cm (3 ft); white-variegated cvs include 'Harlequin', 'Norah Leigh'

Physostegia virginiana 'Variegata' – D, 90 cm (3 ft); white-edged

Plantago asiatica 'Variegata' – D, 20 cm (8 in); grey-green, white-striped

Polygonatum falcatum 'Variegatum' – D, 60 cm (2 ft); white-margined

P. × hybridum 'Striatum' – D, 90 cm (3 ft); ivory-white-streaked

Pulmonaria rubra 'David Ward' – D, 15 cm (6 in); white-margined

Scrophularia auriculata 'Variegata' – D, 90 cm (3 ft); cream-variegated

Sisyrinchium striatum 'Aunt May' – E, 60 cm (2 ft); grey, cream-striped

Soleirolia (syn. *Helxine*) *soleirolii* 'Variegata' – D, 1 cm (½ in); grey-green, white-margined

Symphytum 'Goldsmith' – D, 30 cm (12 in); cream-variegated

S. × uplandicum 'Variegatum' – 1.2 m (4 ft); cream-edged

Thymus × citriodorus 'Silver Queen' – E, 10 cm (4 in); white-variegated

T. vulgaris 'Silver Posie' – E, 15 cm (6 in); white-variegated

Tulbaghia violacea 'Silver Lace' – D, 45 cm (18 in); white-striped

Veronica gentianoïdes 'Variegata' – D, 45 cm (18 in); cream-splashed

Grasses, sedges and bamboos

Arrhenantherum elatius ssp. *bulbosum* 'Variegatum' – D, 30 cm (12 in); white-striped

Arundo donax 'Variegata' – D, 2.4 m (8 ft); ivory-striped

Carex conica 'Snowline' – E, 15 cm (6 in); white-edged

Carex ornithopoda 'Variegata' – D, 15 cm (6 in); pure-white-margined

C. riparia 'Variegata' – D, 60 cm (2 ft); white, thinly green-margined

C. siderosticha 'Variegata' – D, 30 cm (12 in); ivory-striped

Dactylis glomerata 'Variegata' – D, 15 cm (6 in); white-striped

Holcus mollis 'Variegatus' – D, 20 cm (8 in); white-striped

Miscanthus sinensis 'Variegatus' – D, 1.2 m (4 ft); white-striped

Molinia caerulea 'Variegata' – D, 30 cm (12 in); cream-striped

Phalaris arundinacea 'Picta' – D, 90 cm (3 ft); white-striped

P. arundinacea 'Feesey' – D, 90 cm (3 ft); more strongly white-variegated

Pleioblastus variegatus (syn. *Arundinaria fortunei*) – D, 90 cm (3 ft) bamboo; white-striped

Annuals and biennials

Euphorbia marginata – annual, 30 cm (12 in); heavily white-variegated

Silybum marianum – annual, 60 cm (2 ft); white-veined and white-marbled

Tropaeolum majus 'Alaska' – annual, 25 cm (10 in); white-spotted

PLANTS WITH COPPERY AND PURPLE FOLIAGE

Trees

Acacia baileyana 'Purpurea' – E, 4.5 m (15 ft); purple-glaucous

Acer platanoïdes 'Crimson King' – D, 18 m (60 ft); dark purple

Betula pendula 'Purpurea' – D, 9 m (30 ft); dark purple

Catalpa × *erubescens* 'Purpurea' – D, 15 m (50 ft); very dark purple when young

Cercis canadensis 'Forest Pansy' – D, 4.5 m (15 ft); purple

Cordyline australis – E, to 4.5 m (15 ft); purple in Purpurea group, 'Torbay Red'

Fagus sylvatica – D, 27 m (90 ft); copper or purple forms and cvs include 'Riversii' (very dark purple), 'Rohanii', 'Dawyck Purple', 'Purpurea Pendula'

Gleditsia triacanthos 'Rubylace' – D, 9 m (30 ft); red-purple aging to bronzed green

Malus × *purpurea* – D, 4.5 m (15 ft); purple cvs maturing to bronze include 'Aldenhamensis', 'Eleyi', 'Lemoinei'

M. 'Royalty' – D, 4.5 m (15 ft); intense red-purple

Prunus x *blireana* – D, 4.5 m (15 ft); metallic purple

Prunus cerasifera – D, 7 m (25 ft); 'Nigra' very dark purple, 'Pissardii' deep red aging to purple

Shrubs

Acer palmatum – D, 1.5 m (5-13 ft); purple forms and cvs include *atropurpureum*, 'Bloodgood', 'Burgundy Lace', 'Crimson Queen', 'Dissectum Atropurpureum', 'Dissectum Nigrum', 'Garnet', 'Inaba Shidare'

Berberis × *ottawensis* 'Superba' – D, 2.1 m (7 ft); dark maroon-purple

B. × *stenophylla* 'Claret Cascade' – E, 1.2 m (4 ft); wine purple

B. thunbergii – D, 60cm–2.1 m (2-7 ft); purple cvs include *atropurpurea*, 'Atropurpurea Nana', 'Bagatelle', 'Dart's Red Lady', 'Helmond Pillar', 'Red Chief', 'Red Pillar', 'Golden Ring' purple, thinly yellow-margined

Brachyglottis repanda 'Purpurea' – E, 1.5 m (5 ft); black-purple with white reverse

Coprosma 'Coppershine' – E, 1.8 m (6 ft); polished, coppery bronze

Corylus maxima 'Purpurea' – D, 3 m (10 ft); large, black-purple

Cotinus coggygria – D, 2.4 m (8 ft); chocolate brown to maroon-purple forms and cvs include Rubrifolius group, 'Royal Purple', 'Velvet Cloak'

Cotinus 'Grace' – D, 3 m (10 ft); maroon

Diervilla sessilifolia – D, 90 cm (3 ft); milk-chocolate brown

D. × *splendens* – D, 75 cm (2½ ft); coppery bronze

Dodonaea viscosa 'Purpurea' – E, 3 m (10 ft); red-purple

Hebe 'Mrs Winder' ('Waikiki') – E, 90 cm (3 ft); bronze-purple

Leptospermum scoparium 'Nicholsii' – E, 1.8 m (6 ft); purple

Osmanthus heterophyllus 'Purpureus' – E, 1.5 m (5 ft); glossy purple fading to purplish green

Pittosporum tenuifolium 'Purpureum' – E, 2.4 m (8 ft); metallic purple

P. tenuifolium 'Tom Thumb' – E, 90 cm (3 ft); dark metallic purple

Prunus x *cistena* – D, 1.2 m

(4 ft); rich red-purple

Rhododendron 'Elizabeth
Lockhart' – E, 90 cm (3 ft);
chocolate-purple

Rosa glauca – D, 2.4 m (8 ft);
glaucous blue, purple-
flushed in sun

Salvia officinalis 'Purpurascens' –
E, 30 cm (12 in); grey-
purple

Sambucus nigra 'Guincho
Purple' ('Purpurea') – D,
2.1 m (7 ft); purple

Weigela florida 'Foliis Purpureis'
– D, 1.5 m (5 ft); muted
purple

Climbers

Parthenocissus henryana – D,
4.5 m (15 ft); purple-green,
silver veins

Vitis vinifera 'Purpurea' – D,
4.5 m (15 ft); grey-bloomed
purple

Perennials

Aeonium arboreum
'Atropurpureum' – E, 90 cm
(3 ft); mahogany-purple

A. 'Zwartkop' – E, 90 cm
(3 ft); black-purple

Ajuga reptans – E, 10 cm (4 in);
purple or bronze cvs include
'Atropurpurea', 'Braunherz',
'Caitlin's Giant', 'Pink
Surprise'

Anthriscus sylvestris
'Ravenswing' – D, 45 cm
(18 in); bronze deepening to
purple-black

Artemisia kitadakensis 'Guizhou'
– D, 1.2 m (4 ft); black-
green

Canna hybrids – D, 1.2 m
(4 ft); purple cvs include

'Wyoming', 'Roi Humbert'

C. indica 'Purpurea' – D, 1.2 m
(4 ft); purple-maroon

Cimicifuga simplex Atropurpurea
group – D, 1.5 m (5 ft);
chocolate-purple; 'Brunette'
is extra-dark

Clematis recta 'Purpurea' – D,
1.5 m (5 ft); dusky purple

Crocosmia x *crocosmiiflora*
'Solfaterre' – D, 60 cm (2 ft);
chocolate-bronze

Dahlia 'Bishop of Llandaff' –
D, 90 cm (3 ft); metallic
black-maroon

Euphorbia amygdaloïdes 'Rubra'
– SE or E, 30 cm (12 in);
maroon-purple

E. dulcis 'Chameleon' – D,
30 cm (12 in); rich purple

Foeniculum vulgare 'Purpureum'
– D, 1.5 m (5 ft); bronze-
purple

Geranium sessiliflorum
'Nigrescens' – D, 5 cm
(2 in); chocolate brown

Hedychium greenei – D, 1.2 m
(4 ft); mahogany reverse

Heuchera micrantha 'Palace
Purple' – E, 60 cm (2 ft);
dark purple

Hieracium maculatum – D,
10 cm (4 in); bronze-purple
turning blue-grey with dark
brown blotches

Ligularia dentata – 1.2 m (4 ft);
bronzed green, rich maroon
reverse

Lobelia – D, 75 cm (2½ ft);
border cvs with beetroot-
purple foliage include 'Bees
Flame', 'Dark Crusader',
'Queen Victoria'

Lychnis × *arkwrightii* – D, 45 cm
(18 in); dark chocolate

brown

Lysimachia ciliata – D, 75 cm
(2½ ft); milk-chocolate
brown

Oenothera fruticosa 'Fyrverkeri'
['Fireworks'] – D, 45 cm
(18 in); mahogany-purple

Ophiopogon planiscapus
'Nigrescens' – E, 15 cm
(6 in); black

Phormium 'Bronze Baby' – E,
60 cm (2 ft); purple-bronze

P. 'Dark Delight' – E, 90 cm
(3 ft); dark, oxblood red

P. tenax Purpureum group – E,
1.5 m (5 ft); purple-bronze

P. 'Thumbelina' – E, 30 cm
(12 in); dark purple

Plantago major 'Rubrifolia' – D,
20 cm (8 in); red-purple

Primula 'Guinevere' – D,
15 cm (6 in); smoky
bronze

Ranunculus ficaria 'Brazen
Hussy' – D, 10 cm (4 in);
near-black

Rodgersia podophylla – D, 75 cm
(2½ ft); bronzed in sun

Saxifraga fortunei 'Wada' – D,
30 cm (12 in); purple-
maroon

Sedum spathulifolium
'Purpureum' – E, 7 cm
(3 in); purple

S. spurium 'Purpurteppich'
['Purple Carpet'] – E, 7 cm
(3 in); maroon-purple

S. telephium ssp. *maximum*
'Atropurpureum' – D,
60 cm (2 ft); dark bloomy
purple

S. 'Vera Jameson' – D, 15 cm
(6 in); glaucous purple

Sempervivum tectorum – E, 7 cm
(3 in); some purple or

bronze

Tradescantia pallida (Setcreasea) 'Purple Heart' – D, 15 cm (6 in); purple sheened with silver

Trifolium repens 'Purpurascens' – D, carpeter; chocolate-purple, green margined; 'Purpurascens Quadrifolium' four-leaved version

Viola riviniana (syn. *V. labradorica*) Purpurea group – E, 15 cm (6 in); purple

Grasses and sedges

Carex buchananii – E, 60 cm (2 ft); bronze and coppery red

C. comans bronze form – E, 30 cm (12 in); bronze to blonde

C. flagellifera – E, 45 cm (18 in); bronze

C. petriei – E, 30 cm (12 in); pinkish bronze

Imperata cylindrica 'Rubra' – D, 30 cm (12 in); blood red

Miscanthus sinensis var. *purpurascens* – D, 1.2 m (4 ft); upper surface warm brown with pink central vein

Schoenus pauciflorus – E, 45 cm (18 in); maroon

Uncinia egmontiana – E, 15 cm (6 in); bright maroon-red

U. rubra – E, 15 cm (6 in); bright maroon-red

U. uncinata – E, 15 cm (6 in); maroon

Annuals and biennials

Atriplex hortensis var. *rubra* – 1.2 m (4 ft); blood red

Iresine herbstii – 45 cm (18 in); deep red-purple

I. lindenii – 30 cm (12 in); deep beetroot-purple

Ocimum basilicum 'Dark Opal' – 45 cm (18 in); black-purple

Perilla frutescens var. *nankinensis* – 90 cm (3 ft); bronze-purple

Ricinus communis – 1.5 m (5 ft); 'Gibsonii' coppery purple; 'Carmencita' plum-red; 'Impala' bronze-green on red stems

A small grove of maples, chiefly the Japanese Acer palmatum, *show their colours in autumn. With a handful of seed and a few years' patience, a group such as this could be recreated at little cost.*

PLANTS WITH MULTI-COLOURED FOLIAGE

Trees

Acer negundo 'Flamingo' – D, 4.5 m (15 ft); pink maturing to green variegated pink and white

A. pseudoplatanus 'Leopoldii' – D, 18 m (60 ft); yellowish pink maturing to yellow- and pink-splashed green

Cordyline australis 'Albertii' – E, 4.5 m (15 ft); cream-, red- and green-striped

Cornus florida 'Welchii' ('Tricolor') – D, 4.5 m (15 ft); green and white, rose-pink-edged

Crataegus laevigata 'Gireoudii' – D, 4.5 m (15 ft); cream- and pink-mottled

Fagus sylvatica 'Purpurea Tricolor' – D, 12 m (40 ft); purple, pale pink-margined

Ligustrum lucidum 'Tricolor' – E, 6 m (20 ft); white-margined, pink-flushed

Populus × *candicans* 'Aurora' – D, 12 m (40 ft); cream- and pink-splashed

Shrubs

Acer palmatum 'Asahi-zuru' – D, 3 m (10 ft); green, pink and white

A. palmatum 'Dissectum Variegatum' – D, 1.5 m (5 ft); purple, rose-, pink- and cream-margined

Berberis × *ottawensis* 'Silver Mile' – D, 1.8 m (6 ft); purple, silver-splashed

B. × *stenophylla* 'Pink Pearl' – E, 1.2 m (4 ft); pink- and cream-variegated on green

B. thunbergii – D, 90 cm (3 ft); multi-coloured cvs include 'Harlequin', pink, red and creamy yellow; 'Rose Glow' pink and cream on purple

Calluna vulgaris 'Mrs Pat' – E, 20 cm (8 in); shoots tipped pink, coral and scarlet in summer

Cleyera fortunei – E, 1.5 m (5 ft); cream- and pink-margined

Coprosma repens 'Pink Splendour' – E, 60 cm (2 ft); yellow-margined fading to cream, bright pink-flushed

Cornus mas 'Aureoelegantissima' – D, 2.4 m (8 ft); yellow-margined, pink-flushed

Erica carnea 'Ann Sparkes' – E, 25 cm (10 in); orange-yellow, bronze-red-tipped

E. cinerea 'Fiddler's Gold' – E, 25 cm (10 in); yellow, pink-tinted

Fuchsia magellanica 'Versicolor' – D, 1.2 m (4 ft); pink and grey

Hebe 'Amanda Cook' – E, 60 cm (2 ft); cream, green-striped in centre, purple-flushed

H. speciosa 'Tricolor' – E, 90 cm (3 ft); cream, green and blackcurrant purple

Hypericum × *moserianum* 'Tricolor' – D, 60 cm (2 ft); white-, pink- and green-variegated

Leucothoë fontanesiana 'Rainbow' – E, 60 cm (2 ft); cream-, pink-, bronze- and yellow-splashed

Nandina domestica 'Firepower' – E, 90 cm (3 ft); cream, orange and red

Osmanthus heterophyllus 'Goshiki' ('Tricolor') – E, 1.5 m (5 ft); glossy green, white and coral pink

Photinia davidiana 'Palette' – E, 1.8 m (6 ft); red, turning green, pink and white

Pittosporum 'Garnettii' – E, 3 m (10 ft); cream-variegated, rose-red-spotted

P. tenuifolium 'Wendle Channon' – E, 3 m (10 ft); lime yellow, red-tinted

Pseudowintera colorata – E, 1.2 m

(4 ft); metallic yellow with
pink and purple, glaucous-
white reverse

Pyracantha 'Harlequin' – E,
1.5 m (5 ft); cream, pink and
green

Salix integra 'Hakuro-nishiki' –
D, 3 m (10 ft); salmon-pink
new shoots maturing to
pink, white and green

Salvia officinalis 'Tricolor' – E,
60 cm (2 ft); grey, purple
and cream

Spiraea 'Pink Ice' – D, 1.2 m
(4 ft); pink and cream new
foliage maturing to cream
and green

Stachyurus chinensis 'Magpie' – D,
2.1 m (7 ft); cream-margined,
pink-tinged on green

Climbers

Actinidia kolomikta – D, 4.5 m
(15 ft); half green, half cream
and pink

Ampelopsis brevipedunculata
'Elegans' – D, 1.2 m (4 ft);
heavily cream- and pink-
marbled and splashed

Trachelospermum jasminoïdes
'Variegatum' – E, 3 m
(10 ft); cream- and crimson-
pink-variegated

Perennials

Ajuga reptans 'Burgundy Glow'
– E, 10 cm (4 in); magenta,
rose and cream

A. reptans 'Delight' – E, 10 cm
(4 in); pink, grey and cream

A. reptans 'Multicolor' (syn.
'Rainbow') – E, 10 cm
(4 in); bronze, pink, yellow
and cream

Houttuynia cordata 'Chameleon'
– D, 30 cm (12 in); yellow,
red, copper, pink and green

Persicaria (syn. *Polygonum*)
capitata – D, carpeting;
crimson-pink in sun, with
dark chevron

P. (syn. *Tovara*) *virginiana*
'Painter's Palette' – D,
45 cm (18 in); creamy-
yellow-striped with
mahogany chevron

Phormium cookianum 'Tricolor'
– E, 1.2 m (4 ft); cream,
green-striped and red-edged

P. 'Dazzler' – E, 75 cm (2½ ft);
chocolate and blood red,
rose-striped

P. 'Maori Chief' – E, 1.2 m
(4 ft); rose, coral, tan and
bronze

P. 'Maori Maiden' – E, 90 cm
(3 ft); rosy salmon, coral-
striped

P. 'Maori Queen' – E, 90 cm
(3 ft); rose-striped on bronze

P. 'Maori Sunrise' – E, 75 cm
(2½ ft); pink red, bronze-
margined

P. 'Sundowner' – E, 1.8 m
(6 ft); rose-, apricot-, bronze-
and chocolate-striped

Grasses and sedges

Glyceria maxima var. *variegata* –
D, 60 cm (2 ft); cream-
striped, pink at first

Annuals, biennials and tropicals

Amaranthus 'Tricolor
Splendens' – 60 cm (2 ft);
scarlet, yellow and green

Begonia – rex begonias often
silver- and pink-variegated

Caladium – 37 cm (15 in); red,
rose, pink, white and green
in varying combinations

Coleus – 30-60 cm (1-2 ft);
lime, orange, red, purple,
etc.

Cordyline fruticosa (terminalis) –
E, 2.4 m (8 ft); cvs with
bright pink, red or crimson
variegations

Dracaena – E, various; many cvs
with colourful variegations

Iresine herbstii 'Aureoreticulata'
– 30 cm (12 in); yellow, red-
veined

I. herbstii 'Brilliantissima' –
30 cm (12 in); purple, bright
red-veined

Pelargonium – zonal cvs often
yellow- and red-variegated

Zea mays 'Quadricolor' – 1.2 m
(4 ft); pink-, red- and
cream-variegated

PLANTS WITH COLOURED SPRING FOLIAGE

Trees

Acer cappadocicum 'Aureum' – D, 9 m (30 ft); red, turning yellow

A. cappadocicum 'Rubrum' – D, 9 m (30 ft); blood red

A. pseudoplatanus 'Brilliantissimum' – D, 4.5 m (15 ft); shrimp pink and coral, then creamy green

A. pseudoplatanus 'Prinz Handjery' – D, 4.5 m (15 ft); shrimp pink and coral, then green with purple reverse

Aesculus neglecta 'Erythroblastos' – D, 4.5 m (15 ft); coral red

Cercidiphyllum japonicum – D, 6 m (20 ft); claret and pink

Eucalyptus niphophila – E, 6 m (20 ft); red, coral and maroon

Koelreuteria paniculata – D, 9 m (30 ft); pink and bronze

Prunus – D, 6 m (20 ft); Japanese cherries with coloured spring foliage include 'Fugenzo' (rich copper), 'Choshu-hizakura' ('Hisakura') (coppery-red), 'Hokusai' (bronze-brown), 'Jo-nioi' (golden-bronze), 'Kursar' (red-bronze), 'Pandora' (bronze-red), 'Shirofugen' (copper), 'Tai Haku' (bright red-bronze), 'Ukon' (bronze)

P. jamasakura (syn. *P. serrulata* var. *spontanea*) – D, 6 m (20 ft); coppery red

P. sargentii – D, 6 m (20 ft); bronze-red

Sorbus aria 'Lutescens' – D, 6 m (20 ft); velvety, ivory

S. cashmeriana – D, 4.5 m (15 ft); deep crimson-pink

Toona (syn. *Cedrela*) *sinensis* 'Flamingo' – D, 6 m (20 ft); bright coral red

Shrubs

Acer palmatum – D, 3 m (10 ft); cvs with coloured spring foliage include 'Corallinum' (coral pink), 'Osakazuki' (scarlet), 'Katsura' (orange-buff and red); 'Shindeshojo' (scarlet), 'Shishio' (red)

Aesculus parviflora – D, 3.5 m (12 ft); bronzed

Camellia cuspidata – E, 1.8 m (6 ft); copper to near-black

Corylopsis pauciflora – D, 1.2 m (4 ft); coral and pink

C. willmottiae 'Spring Purple' – D, 1.8 m (6 ft); bloomy purple

Fothergilla gardenii 'Blue Mist' – D, 60 cm (2 ft); powder blue then blue-green

Hamamelis vernalis 'Sandra' – D, 2.4 m (8 ft); plum purple

Leucothoë 'Scarletta' – E, 30 cm (12 in); bright red

Nandina domestica – E, 3 m (10 ft); red to bronze-pink

Nyssa sinensis – D, 4.5 m (15 ft); young foliage red all spring and summer

Photinia × fraseri – E, 4.5 m (15 ft); sealing-wax red cvs include 'Red Robin', 'Birmingham', 'Robusta', 'Redstart', 'Rubens'

Pieris 'Bert Chandler' – E, 1.2 m (4 ft); yellow or red

P. 'Firecrest' – E, 1.5 m (5 ft) scarlet fading to coral and peach to lemon and green

P. 'Forest Flame' – E, 1.5 m (5 ft); scarlet fading to coral, cream and green

P. formosa 'Charles Michael' – E, 1.8 m (6 ft); scarlet

P. formosa Forrestii group – E, 1.8 m (6 ft); scarlet fading to coral, lemon and green

P. formosa 'Jermyns' – E, 1.2 m (4 ft); grenadier scarlet

P. formosa 'Wakehurst' – E, 1.8 m (6 ft); sealing-wax red fading through shrimp and primrose to green

P. japonica 'Flaming Silver' – E, 1.5 m (5 ft); bright red then green, white-edged

P. japonica 'Grayswood' – E, 1.5 m (5 ft); bronze

P. japonica 'Mountain Fire' – E, 1.5 m (5 ft); deep red

P. japonica 'Purity' – E, 1.5 m (5 ft); red-bronze

P. japonica 'Scarlett O'Hara' – E, 1.5 m (5 ft); red

P. japonica 'Tilford' – E, 1.5 m (5 ft); bright crimson-red

Rhododendron 'Bow Bells' – E, 1.2 m (4 ft); bright copper

R. cinnabarinum – E, 1.5 m (5 ft); glaucous foliage, intensely blue in spring

R. lutescens – E, 1.8 m (6 ft); coppery red

R. 'Moser's Maroon' – E, 2.4 m (8 ft); dark maroon-purple

R. williamsianum – E, 90 cm (3 ft); chocolate brown

R. 'Winsome' – E, 1.2 m (4 ft); copper

R. yakushimanum – E, 90 cm (3 ft); silver-felted

Spiraea japonica – D, 75 cm (2½ ft); lime-yellow cvs, bright copper in spring, include 'Goldflame', 'Gold Mound', 'Golden Princess'

Vaccinium floribundum – E, 90 cm (3 ft); mahogany red

V. moupinense – E, 30 cm (12 in); golden brown

V. ovatum – E, 1.8 m (6 ft); coppery mahogany

Viburnum sargentii 'Onandaga' – D, 2.4 m (8 ft); plum purple

Conifers

Chamaecyparis lawsoniana 'Silver Queen' – E, 3 m (10 ft); silver-green, creamy white in spring

C. lawsoniana 'Snow White' – E, 1.2 m (4 ft); blue-green, white-tipped

C. lawsoniana 'White Spot' – E, 1.8 m (6 ft); white-tipped

C. pisifera 'Squarrosa Sulphurea' – E, 3 m (10 ft); creamy sulphur-grey

Juniperus communis 'Depressa Aurea' – E, 60 cm (2 ft); butter yellow

J. communis 'Golden Showers' – E, 1.5 m (5 ft); gold fading to bronze

J. squamata 'Holger' – E, 30 cm (12 in); creamy yellow

Picea abies 'Aurea' – E, 3 m (10 ft); bright yellow

P. orientalis 'Aurea' – E, 3 m (10 ft); creamy yellow maturing to green

P. orientalis 'Wittboldt' – E, 1.2 m (4 ft); bright creamy gold maturing to green

Thuja orientalis 'Golden Ball' – E, 45 cm (18 in); yellow

Perennials

Astilbe – D, 30-75 cm (1–2½ ft); cvs with mahogany-red spring foliage include 'Bronze Elegance', 'Dunkellachs' (copper) and red-flowered cvs

Astrantia major 'Sunningdale Variegated' – D, 60 cm (2 ft); creamy and green

Dryopteris erythrosora – D, fern, 60 cm (2 ft); copper

Epimedium – D, 20–30 cm (8–12 in); *E.* × *versicolor*, *E.* × *rubrum* and *E. grandiflorum* all tinted bronze or pink

Euphorbia sikkimensis – D, 1.8 m (6 ft); crimson-scarlet

Geranium × *monacense* 'Muldoon' (syn. *G. punctatum*) – D, 30 cm (12 in); primrose yellow, maroon-spotted

Hemerocallis lilioasphodelus and *H. fulva* – D, 90 cm (3 ft); chartreuse

Heuchera americana – D, 45 cm (18 in); coppery mahogany

Hosta fortunei var. *albopicta* – D, 60 cm (2 ft); butter yellow, pale green-edged

H. fortunei aurea – D, 60 cm (2 ft); pale yellow

Iris pseudacorus 'Variegata' – D, 90 cm (3 ft); yellow-striped

Oenothera fruticosa – D, 45 cm (18 in); mahogany

Paeonia lactiflora – D, 90 cm (3 ft); many have rich crimson spring foliage

P. mlokosewitchii – D, 60 cm (2 ft); dove grey and pink

P. obovata var. *alba* – D, 45 cm (18 in); grey-green and copper

Rheum palmatum 'Atrosanguineum' – D, 1.8 m (6 ft); rich crimson

Stachys byzantina 'Primrose Heron' – D, 45 cm (18 in); lime yellow turning silver

Tulipa greigii – D, bulb, 20 cm (8 in); grey-green, dark maroon-purple-striped; also tulip hybrid 'Red Riding Hood'

Valeriana phu 'Aurea' – D, 90 cm (3 ft); bright yellow

PLANTS WITH BRIGHT AUTUMN TINTS

Trees

Acer capillipes – D, 4.5 m (15 ft); vivid red

A. davidii – D, 4.5 m (15 ft); rich crimson

A. griseum – D, 4.5 m (15 ft); crimson and scarlet

A. grosseri var. *hersii* – D, 4.5 m (15 ft); crimson and scarlet

A. japonicum – D, 4.5 m (15 ft); cv 'Aconitifolium' ('Laciniatum', 'Filicifolium') ruby-crimson, 'Vitifolium' scarlet

A. maximowiczianum (syn. *A. nikoense*) – D, 6 m (20 ft); orange and flame

A. palmatum – D, to 4.5 m (15 ft); orange to scarlet and crimson, including. 'Osakazuki', vivid scarlet, 'Senkaki', butter yellow

A. pensylvanicum – D, 4.5 m (15 ft); bright yellow

A. rubrum – D, 18 m (60 ft); rich scarlet; cv 'October Glory' vivid crimson

A. rufinerve – D, 6 m (20 ft); red and yellow

Amelanchier lamarckii – D, 4.5 m (15 ft); flame and scarlet

Betula – D, 12 m (40 ft); most turn golden yellow

Cercidiphyllum japonicum – D, 6 m (20 ft); smoky pink

Cornus controversa – D, 4.5 m (15 ft); purple-red; 'Variegata' pink

C. florida 'Rainbow' – D, 4.5 m (15 ft); purple, red-edged

C. florida 'Welchii' – ('Tricolor') D, 4.5 m (15 ft); purple, rose-edged

Crataegus persimilis 'Prunifolia' – D, 4.5 m (15 ft); orange and scarlet

Liquidambar styraciflua – D, 15 m (50 ft); varying from orange through scarlet and crimson to oxblood red

Malus tschonoskii – D, 12 m (40 ft); yellow, orange, scarlet and purple

Nyssa sylvatica – D, 12 m (40 ft); scarlet and orange

Parrotia persica – D, 4.5 m (15 ft); crimson and yellow

Prunus sargentii – D, 15 m (50 ft); scarlet and orange

Quercus coccinea – D, 18 m (60 ft); brilliant scarlet

Q. rubra – D, 18 m (60 ft); red

Sassafras albidum – D, 12 m (40 ft); clear yellow

Sorbus cashmeriana – D, 6 m (20 ft); crimson and purple

S. commixta – D, 6 m (20 ft); orange, scarlet and crimson

S. hupehensis – D, 6 m (20 ft); dusky pink and purple

S. 'Joseph Rock' – D, 6 m (20 ft); orange and purple

S. sargentiana – D, 9 m (30 ft); rich red

S. scalaris – D, 6 m (20 ft); scarlet and crimson

S. vilmorinii – D, 4.5 m (15 ft); crimson and purple

Stewartia pseudocamellia – D, 6 m (20 ft); red and gold

S. sinensis – D, 4.5 m (15 ft); rich red

Shrubs

Acer circinatum – D, 3 m (10 ft); orange and crimson

A. palmatum – D, 1.5 m (5 ft); 'Dissectum' forms scarlet

A. tataricum ssp. *ginnala* – D, 3 m (10 ft); orange and scarlet crimson

Aesculus parviflora – D, 3.5 m (12 ft); clear yellow

Amelanchier canadensis – D, 3 m (10 ft); flame and scarlet

Aronia arbutifolia 'Brilliant' – D, 1.8 m (6 ft); scarlet

A. melanocarpa – D, 1.2 m (4 ft); scarlet and orange

Berberis dictyophylla – D, 1.8 m (6 ft); scarlet and crimson

B. thunbergii – D, 30 cm–1.8 m (1–6 ft); scarlet

B. wilsoniae – D, 90 cm (3 ft);

coral and scarlet

Callicarpa bodinieri 'Profusion' –
   D, 2.1 m (7 ft); pink and
   purple

Ceratostigma willmottianum – D,
   75 cm (2½ ft); scarlet

Cornus florida – D, 3.5 m
   (12 ft); scarlet and flame

C. kousa – D, 3.5 m (12 ft);
   scarlet and coral

C. sanguinea 'Winter Beauty' –
   D, 1.2 m (4 ft); orange

Cotinus coggygria – D, 3 m
   (10 ft); scarlet and crimson;
   'Flame' cv. scarlet

C. obovatus – D, 4 m (13 ft);
   scarlet and orange

Cotoneaster adpressus – D, 60 cm
   (2 ft); red

C. bullatus – D, 3.5 m (12 ft);
   rich red

C. horizontalis – D, 60 cm
   (2 ft); crimson and scarlet

Disanthus cercidifolius – D, 3 m
   (10 ft); crimson and purple

Enkianthus campanulatus – D,
   3 m (10 ft); yellow, orange,
   scarlet and crimson

E. perulatus – D, 1.8 m (6 ft);
   deep red

Eucryphia glutinosa – D, 4 m
   (12 ft); scarlet and flame

Euonymus alatus – D, 1.8 m
   (6 ft); crimson and scarlet

E. oxyphyllus – D, 1.8 m (6 ft);
   ruby and purple

E. planipes – D, 2.4 m (8 ft);
   crimson and scarlet

Fothergilla gardenii – D, 90 cm
   (3 ft); scarlet and orange

F. major – D, 1.2 m (4 ft);
   orange and scarlet

Hamamelis × *intermedia* – D,
   2.4 m (8 ft); yellow to scarlet

H. japonica – D, 2.4 m (8 ft);
yellow

H. mollis – D, 2.4 m (8 ft);
   yellow

H. vernalis 'Sandra' – D, 2.4 m
   (8 ft); orange, scarlet and
   crimson

Hydrangea 'Preziosa' – D, 75
   cm (2½ ft); plum and crimson

H. quercifolia – D, 1.8 m (6 ft);
   vivid scarlet and crimson

Oxydendrum arboreum – D,
   2.4 m (8 ft); orange, scarlet
   and crimson

Parrotia persica – D, 4.5 m
   (15 ft); crimson, scarlet,
   orange and yellow; 'Pendula'
   similar but
   prostrate/weeping

Photinia villosa – D, 2.4 m
   (8 ft); scarlet and gold

Prunus glandulosa – D, 1.2 m
   (4 ft); coral and pink

Rhododendron – D, 1.8-2.4 m
   (6-8 ft); several azaleas,
   including *R. luteum*, orange,
   flame and scarlet

Rhus typhina – D, 2.4 m (8 ft);
   flame, orange and scarlet

Ribes odoratum – D, 1.2 m
   (4 ft); scarlet and crimson

Rosa nitida – D, 60 cm (2 ft);
   brilliant scarlet-crimson

R. rugosa – D, 1.2 m (4 ft);
   straw yellow

R. virginiana – D, 90 cm (3 ft);
   orange, scarlet and red

Spiraea prunifolia – D, 1.8 m
   (6 ft); orange and red

Vaccinium corymbosum – D,
   1.2 m (4 ft); orange, scarlet
   and copper

Viburnum opulus – D, 2.4 m
   (8 ft); red

V. plicatum – D, 1.8 m (6 ft);
   red to plum

Climbers

Parthenocissus henryana – D,
   4.5 m (15 ft); crimson and
   purple

P. quinquefolia – D, 7.5 m
   (25 ft); scarlet and orange

P. tricuspidata – D, 9 m (30 ft);
   scarlet and crimson

Vitis 'Brant' – D, 4.5 m (15 ft);
   crimson and purple, green-
   veined

V. coignetiae – D, 6 m (20 ft);
   scarlet, crimson and purple

Conifers

Ginkgo biloba – D, 6 m (20 ft);
   clear yellow

Metasequoia glyptostroboïdes – D,
   12 m (40 ft); tawny pink

Taxodium distichum – D, 12 m
   (40 ft); orange and bronze

Perennials

Aruncus aethusifolius – D, 30 cm
   (12 in); coral and apricot

Ceratostigma plumbaginoïdes – D,
   30 cm (12 in); scarlet

Chrysanthemum 'Emperor of
   China' – D, 1.2 m (4 ft);
   deep crimson and plum

Geranium macrorrhizum – SE or
   E, 30 cm (12 in); scarlet

Osmunda regalis – D, 1.2 m
   (4 ft); yellow and bronze

Paeonia lactiflora – D, 1.2 m
   (4 ft); orange and flame

Grasses

Miscanthus sinensis var.
   purpurascens – D, 1.2 m (4 ft);
   orange, red and buff

Annuals

Kochia scoparia f. *trichophylla* –
   75 cm (2½ ft); bright red

PLANTS WITH COLOURED WINTER FOLIAGE

Shrubs

Azalea – E, 60 cm (2 ft); many crimson and mahogany

Calluna vulgaris – E, 30 cm (12 in); cvs include 'Blazeaway', rich red; 'Firefly', orange-red; 'Golden Feather', warm orange; 'Joy Vanstone', rich orange; 'Robert Chapman', gold deepening to red; 'Sir John Charrington', orange turning to scarlet and flame; 'Sunset', orange-gold turning bronze; 'Wickwar Flame', orange-yellow deepening to red; 'Winter Chocolate', chocolate-bronze, red in autumn, yellow with pink tips in spring

Cistus × corbariensis – E, 60 cm (2 ft); bronze-purple

Erica carnea 'Foxhollow' – E, 20 cm (8 in); yellow, pink and red

E. cinerea – E, 25 cm (10 in); cvs include 'Windlebrooke', yellow deepening to orange and gold; 'Golden Hue', yellow turning to red

Euphorbia characias spp. *wulfenii* 'Perry's Winter Blusher' – E, 1.2 m (4 ft); maroon-purple

Gaultheria procumbens – E, 15 cm (6 in); mahogany red

Leucothoë fontanesiana – E, 90 cm (3 ft); mahogany red and purple

L. keiskei – E, 60 cm (2 ft); coppery red and bronzed purple

Mahonia aquifolium – E, 75 cm (2½ ft); bronzed

M. nervosa – E, 45 cm (18 in); burnished mahogany

M. × wagneri 'Moseri' – E, 90 cm (3 ft); scarlet, orange and flame

M. × wagneri 'Undulata' – E, 90 cm (3 ft); mahogany purple

Rhododendron PJM hybrids – E, 90 cm (3 ft); red and purple

Vaccinium vitis-idaea – E, carpeting; burnished copper

Climbers

Euonymus fortunei 'Coloratus' – E, 6 m (20 ft); blood red

Hedera helix 'Glymii' – E, 3 m (10 ft); almost black

H. helix 'Tricolor' – E, 3 m (10 ft); cream, pink and purple

Trachelospermum jasminoïdes 'Variegatum' – E, 3.5 m (12 ft); pink and crimson

Conifers

Chamaecyparis thyoïdes 'Ericoides' – E, 90 cm (3 ft); bronze to plum purple

C. thyoïdes 'Rubicon' – E, 60 cm (2 ft); wine red

Cryptomeria japonica 'Compressa' – E, 90 cm (3 ft); red-purple

C. japonica 'Elegans' – E, 4.5 m (15 ft); fox red and bronze-purple

C. japonica 'Elegans Compacta' – E, 1.8 m (6 ft); rich purple

C. japonica 'Vilmoriniana' – E, 90 cm (3 ft); red-purple

Juniperus horizontalis – E, prostrate; cvs bronze or purple in winter include 'Wiltonii', 'Youngstown'

Lepidothamnus laxifolius (syn. *Dacrydium laxifolium*) – E, prostrate; glaucous turning violet-purple

Microbiota decussata – E, prostrate; fox red

Pinus mugo 'Ophir' – E, 60 cm (2 ft); bright gold

P. radiata 'Aurea' – E, 12 m (40 ft); intense golden yellow

P. sylvestris 'Aurea' – E, 4.5 m (15 ft); warm golden yellow

Thuja occidentalis 'Rheingold' –
E, 1.2 m (4 ft); coppery gold
and amber

T. orientalis 'Juniperoïdes' – E,
2.1 m (7 ft); mauve

T. orientalis 'Meldensis' – E,
60 cm (2 ft); plum purple

T. orientalis 'Rosedalis' – E,
60 cm (2 ft); glaucous purple

Thujopsis dolobrata 'Nana' – E,
60 cm (2 ft); coppery orange

Perennials

Bergenia 'Abendglut' – E,
25 cm (10 in); maroon and
plum red

B. 'Ballawley' – E, 60 cm
(2 ft); mahogany purple

B. cordifolia 'Purpurea' – E,
60 cm (2 ft); purplish

B. crassifolia – E, 30 cm (12 in);
mahogany red

B. purpurascens – E, 30 cm
(12 in); beetroot purple, red
reverse

B. 'Sunningdale' – E, 30 cm
(12 in); bronze-purple,
mahogany-red reverse

Galax urceolata (syn. *G. aphylla*)
– E, 30 cm (12 in); glossy,
mahogany red

Heuchera 'Taff's Joy' – E, 30 cm
(12in); cream on grey,
turning rich pink at the
margins

Libertia ixioïdes – E, 60 cm
(2 ft); narrow, orange-tan

L. peregrinans – E, 45 cm
(18 in); narrow, orange

Tellima grandiflora Rubra group
– E, 30 cm (12 in); crimson
and mahogany

Tiarella cordifolia – E, 15 cm
(6 in); lobed, bronzed

T. wherryi – E, 30 cm (12 in);
bronzed

Annuals and biennials

Brassica – E, 20 cm (8 in);
ornamental cabbage and
kale, cream, pink and purple

INDEX

Page numbers in *italics* refer to captions to illustrations